G000144997

Rely on Thomas Cook as your
travelling companion on your next trip
and benefit from our unique heritage.

Thomas Cook **pocket** guides

BORDEAUX
Jane Anson

Thomas
Cook

Written & updated by Jane Anson

Published by Thomas Cook Publishing
A division of Thomas Cook Tour Operations Limited
Company registration No: 3772199 England
The Thomas Cook Business Park, 9 Coningsby Road
Peterborough PE3 8SB, United Kingdom
Email: books@thomascook.com, Tel: +44 (0)1733 416477
www.thomascookpublishing.com

Produced by The Content Works Ltd
Aston Court, Kingsmead Business Park, Frederick Place
High Wycombe, Bucks HP11 1LA
www.thecontentworks.com

Series design based on an original concept by Studio 183 Limited

ISBN: 978-1-84848-300-2

First edition © 2008 Thomas Cook Publishing
This second edition © 2010 Thomas Cook Publishing
Text © Thomas Cook Publishing
Maps © Thomas Cook Publishing/PCGraphics (UK) Limited
Transport map © Communicarta Limited

Series Editor: Kelly Anne Pipes
Production/DTP: Steven Collins

Printed and bound in Spain by GraphyCems

Cover photography (Black grapes on the vine) © Bon Appetit/Alamy

CONTENTS

SYMBOLS KEY

The following symbols are used throughout this book:

ⓐ address   ☎ telephone   ⓦ website address
🄻 opening times   ⓝ public transport connections

The following symbols are used on the maps:

🄸	information office	▪	points of interest
🛫	airport	O	city
✚	hospital	O	large town
🛡	police station	○	small town
🚍	bus station	=	motorway
🚆	railway station	—	main road
✝	cathedral	—	minor road
❶	numbers denote	—	railway
	featured cafés & restaurants		

Hotels and restaurants are graded by approximate price as follows:
£ budget price   **££** mid-range price   **£££** expensive

Abbreviations used in addresses:

av.   avenue
blvd boulevard
pl.   place (square)

▶ *The rooftops, spires and streets of Bordeaux*

INTRODUCING
Bordeaux

Introduction

Bordeaux is the epitome of an elegant French city, with its sweeping, 18th-century waterfront and tree-lined boulevards. Defined by its wine the world over, sometimes it has also been limited by it and written off as snooty and self-important, a verdict that any modern-day visitor would reject. Bordeaux has never been so ripe for a second look. Declared a UNESCO World Heritage Site in 2007, and with almost 350 buildings classified as historic monuments (the only French city to beat this number is Paris), Bordeaux has woken up to the fact that its cultural heritage extends far beyond the grape. It's still rightly known for the quality of its vineyards, of course, but the city is also turning into a culturally vibrant centre, with a sleek new tram system and spruced up quays lining either side of the Garonne River with parks, restaurants and bars.

Today's Bordeaux is also one of the high-tech centres of France, with 20,000 people employed in the aeronautical industry. Its position on the Atlantic coast, just a few hours from the Spanish border, makes its chic resorts increasingly attractive to growing numbers of visitors. The river banks of the Garonne, deep enough to welcome cruise ships right into the centre of the city, still see the arrival and departure of millions of tonnes of goods each year, and the city centre boasts the longest pedestrianised shopping street in Europe. Bordeaux is a surprising city to visit in many ways. Put aside those out-of-date expectations, and a few days' exploration will show why UNESCO described the city as a 'melting pot of humanism, universality and culture'.

🔺 *Just one of Bordeaux's numerous* caves à vin *(wine cellars)*

When to go

Bordeaux offers something for visitors year round. In summer, you are only half an hour from the beaches of Arcachon and the Atlantic Coast, with its many surfing resorts, while in the city centre the Miroir d'Eau (see page 61) provides hours of splashing opportunities. In winter, there are the truffles of Périgord in the Dordogne region an hour to the east, plus the restaurants, theatre and Christmas market of the city centre.

SEASONS & CLIMATE
The city of Bordeaux is only 80 km (50 miles) inland from the Atlantic Ocean, on the Garonne River. The Gulf Stream passes right by, which means mild temperatures through most of the year, and few extremes. Average temperatures range from 10°–30°C (50°–86°F), with a few freezing periods in winter, and some days in summer when it may climb up to 40°C (104°F).

ANNUAL EVENTS
The events scene in Bordeaux is just getting better and better. Despite the inevitable focus on wine, the city is making increasingly louder bleeps on the radar of a wider cultural agenda.

January & February
Jumping International The Bordeaux region is known for its show-jumping events, and this is the largest of the year, held at

Bordeaux Lac in the first week of the month. 🕿 (05) 56 11 99 00
🌐 www.bordeaux-expo.com/jumping 🅽 Bus: 31

May

Garden Festival All the city's parks open up and hold special
events all month, from dance and opera to children's theatre.
🅰 Hôtel de Ville (Bordeaux Town Hall), pl. Pey-Berland
🕿 (05) 56 10 20 30

Union des Grand Crus Wine Weekend For one weekend
(check website for dates), the region's top wine châteaux

⬥ *The Fête du Vin is Europe's largest wine festival*

hold tastings for the general public in central Bordeaux.
ⓐ 10 cours du 30 Juillet **ⓣ** (05) 56 51 91 91 **ⓦ** www.ugcb.net

June–August

Bordeaux Pride On the first Saturday in June, the gay pride
festival holds its Bordeaux bash, with a colourful procession
and party. **ⓦ** www.lgpbordeaux.net

Les Épicuriales Annual food festival held from the end of June
(and into July) in the allées de Tourny, with a variety of the
world's cuisines. **ⓣ** (05) 56 00 66 00

Les Estivales du Musique (Summer Music) Various classical
concerts take place all summer in châteaux around the Médoc.
ⓐ Tourist office, 12 cours du 30 juillet **ⓣ** (05) 56 00 66 00
ⓦ www.estivales-musique-medoc.com

Fête du Vin Europe's biggest wine festival, with each of the
producers setting up tasting stands around the place des
Quinconces and the river banks. **ⓣ** (05) 56 00 66 00
ⓦ www.bordeaux-fete-le-vin.com

September

Journées du Patrimoine On the third weekend of the month
many monuments and historic homes open to the public.
ⓣ (05) 56 00 66 00 **ⓦ** www.bordeaux-tourisme.com

November

Novart A cultural festival with various artists, musicians
and street performers staging events throughout
the city, many of which are free. **ⓣ** (05) 56 10 20 46
ⓦ www.bordeaux.fr

December

Christmas Fair Wooden huts and stalls set up around allées de Tourny selling Christmas decorations, presents and trees.
☎ (05) 56 00 66 00 🌐 www.bordeaux-tourisme.com

PUBLIC HOLIDAYS
Jour de l'An (New Year's Day) 1 Jan
Lundi de Pâques (Easter Monday) 25 Apr 2011, 9 Apr 2012, 1 Apr 2013
Fête du Travail (Labour Day) 1 May
Victoire 1945 (World War II Armistice) 8 May
Ascension 2 June 2011, 17 May 2012, 9 May 2013
Lundi de Pentecôte (Whit Monday) 13 June 2011, 28 May 2012, 20 May 2013
Bastille Day/Fête Nationale (French Revolution) 14 July
Assomption (Assumption) 15 Aug
Toussaint (All Saints' Day) 1 Nov
Armistice 1918 (World War I Armistice) 11 Nov
Noël (Christmas Day) 25 Dec

On these days government departments, banks, shops and even some restaurants are closed.

Wine

Bordeaux is one of the world capitals of wine. The extent of the industry is huge: there are approximately 12,000 winemakers, 8,000 châteaux and 400 wine merchants – not to mention the number of barrel makers, bottle makers, bureaucrats and bar staff – in the Bordeaux area; indeed four out of every ten adults here work in the wine industry in some capacity.

The history of wine in this part of France stretches back over 2,000 years, to when the Romans were planting an ancestor of today's Cabernet Sauvignon grape. Today, there are red, white and rosé (sometimes called *clairet*) wines available, plus a local sparkling wine known as *crémant*. Bordeaux (the wine, not the place) has an unfortunate reputation for being confusing: there are 57 appellations (or regions), and each produces different styles that are bottled and given labels that show the classification, the village, the winemaker... but not the grape. This is because Bordeaux is a blended wine.

The main grape varieties used for blending are actually very well known – Cabernet Sauvignon and Merlot for the reds, Sauvignon Blanc and Semillon for the whites. (In fact 33 per cent of the world's Merlot is grown here, and almost 15 per cent of its Sauvignon Blanc.) The wines from the Left Bank (the Médoc) tend to be richer, longer-lasting and heavier, while those from the Right Bank (Saint Émilion, Pomerol) are more feminine, rounded and can be drunk younger.

Fairs that sell local wines are held locally throughout the year, but before heading out to the vineyards, one of the best ways to get to grips with the subject is to visit the École du Vin (see page 76) for a short introduction, or even the wine bar at the **CIVB** (Bar à Vin, Conseil Interprofessionnel du Vin de Bordeaux ⓐ 3 cours du 30 juillet ⓣ (05) 56 00 43 47 ⓛ 10.00–21.00), where they serve glasses of most different regions, and provide maps, books and magazines on the vineyards to peruse while you're having a drink.

◗ *Bordeaux's vineyards are among the most important in France*

History

Like most river cities, Bordeaux's story is long and varied.
Its proximity to the Atlantic Ocean, coupled with the security
offered by its deep, inland harbour, has made it an attractive
proposition to settlers for millennia. There are remains of
Neanderthal man at the Pair-non-Pair grotto among the
vineyards of Premières Côtes de Blaye, and the district of
Saint Pierre – today the perfect spot for antiques hunting
on a Sunday morning – is located on the exact site of the
Roman port of Burdigala.

But it was the commercial links with Britain and northern
Europe, forged in earnest after the 12th century when Eleanor
of Aquitaine married King Henry II, that saw the city (and its
wines) really prosper. After the French victory over the English
at Castillon in 1453, the city was united again with France
(it had spent a while under English rule), and the focus of
trade switched from England to France and northern Europe.

The safe harbour made Bordeaux ideal for trading. In the
18th century it was one of France's wealthiest commercial centres,
with the quays of the Chartrons district busy with wine traders
from Ireland, Scotland and Holland vying for space in large
warehouses storing wood, sugar, coffee and spices from
France's colonies. The sweeping line of stone façades,
elaborately carved arches and sloping slate roofs along the
river front remains almost unchanged, attesting to the wealth
of the period. Many of the buildings were designed by Paris's
architect, Baron Georges Haussmann.

RESISTANCE BORDEAUX

Although the city was occupied during World War II (and was the scene of the armistice with the Germans in 1940), it also fostered significant pockets of Resistance. The fascinating Centre Jean Moulin (see page 64) examines the Resistance movement without shirking from confronting the extent of collaboration (on display there's some rather terrifying Nazi memorabilia aimed at convincing the French to stand shoulder to shoulder with the invading army). The museum is named after Jean Moulin, whose sympathies with the Resistance movement forced him into exile in England, from where he coordinated operations and organised a secret army. Parachuted into Provence, he worked for the Resistance until he was finally arrested at Caluire on 21 June 1943. Having been tortured, he died during his transfer from France to Germany.

Bordeaux in the 1970s and 1980s was heavily industrial – the now-gleaming waterfront was down-at-heel, and the Right Bank languished as an industrial desert. In recent years, the city has been the focus of much regeneration, especially since Mayor Alain Juppé came to office in the late 1990s (see Culture, page 20). Twenty-first century Bordeaux is a city that's ready to use the best traditions of its past to equip it for the challenges of the future.

Lifestyle

Some of the clichés associated with Bordeaux – that it is a more reserved city than southern centres such as Marseilles, Nice or Cannes, and that its residents tend to be fairly closed off to newcomers – remain apposite. Perhaps it's something to do with the historical links with the British and northern Europeans, but the Bordelais – to give them their correct name – do tend to dress very smartly, stick to fairly strict social rules, and project an image of being a little closed (at first) to visitors. But increasingly they are embracing their southern French side and – especially if you try speaking a little French – they are very friendly and genuinely happy to welcome you. Some of them are getting used to the new, more glamorous Bordeaux just as much as you are.

The best way to soak up the revitalised lifestyle of Bordeaux is along the quays on a summer day, when the whole city seems to have moved outside, rollerblading or strolling along the river, enjoying the many bars, restaurants and markets there.

The cost of living is fairly reasonable, and cheaper than Paris or London, but it's still a big city, so you do pay a premium. Smoking is widespread, though it's now officially banned in public places such as bars, cafés and restaurants.

Despite its many churches, Bordeaux is not a particularly religious city. However, Sundays appear to be almost sacrosanct, with very few shops open and many bars and restaurants also closing up for the day. About the only shops that do open on a Sunday are bakeries and pharmacies, so be aware of this before planning your souvenir shopping. Luckily, many museums do open on a Sunday, often closing on a Monday instead.

🔺 *A pleasant shopping street in Bordeaux*

Culture

There are many sides to Bordeaux's cultural life: the more traditional aspect has over 20 museums and such institutions as the Grand Théâtre (see page 81) and the medieval courtyard that is the city's most picturesque summer gallery, **Cour Mably** (❷ 3 rue Mably ❶ (05) 56 00 66 00); there is plenty of popular culture, too, from live music in the CAPC Musée d'Art Contemporain (Museum of Contemporary Art, see page 80), to festivals such as the Fête du Vin (see Annual events, page 10). Many events are based around wine – look out for 'Portes Ouvertes' (open door) weekends (see ❿ www.bordeaux-tourisme.com for details), when wine co-operatives stage cultural entertainments and tastings.

Smaller spaces include the Frac Gallery (see page 80), the Base Sous-Marine (see page 79), the Cortex Athletico Gallery (see page 64) and the Jardin Botanique (see page 93) in the Bastide.

There are various summer festivals in many of the smaller towns and villages around Bordeaux, such as **Jazz Fort-Médoc** (❶ (05) 56 58 91 30), staged in the ruins of Fort Vauban in Cussac-Fort-Médoc. The festival is held on the third weekend of July and consists of two days of musical eclecticism.

Don't think for a minute that the city's cultural visage is that of the fey aesthete. The relish with which the locals hurl themselves into the annual re-enactment of their humiliation of the English at the battle of Castillon (see page 118), and their prolongation of the celebrations over several weekends, amounts to a good-natured gloat-fest that typifies the Bordelais' inclusive, expansive attitude to celebrating their culture.

🔺 *An exhibition of diverse sculpture at Cour Mably*

REGENERATION BORDEAUX

The 21st century has so far seen Bordeaux undergo a major renovation, an ongoing project started largely by the Mayor, Alain Juppé, and co-financed by the European Regional Development Fund. Its aim is to regenerate the riverside area using an integrated set of measures involving urban renewal, economic investment and social and cultural development. This has so far resulted in the building of the new tramway, new underground parking, the regeneration of the Right Bank, the planting of parks along the river, large swathes of pedestrianised footways, the sandblasting of all the buildings along the waterfront and the reclamation of the Bassins à Flot and the Marina. The new tram line is now complete and another one is planned for 2015 to join the suburbs of Le Bouscat and Cauderan. 2014 will see a brand new bridge crossing the Garonne at the Bacalan end of the city. Plans for the Marina remain on the drawing board, but residents agree that the city has already changed beyond all recognition.

◉ *The wide pavements and spruced up buildings along the riverside*

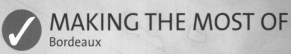

MAKING THE MOST OF
Bordeaux

Shopping

Shopping opportunities in Bordeaux have multiplied recently. For clothes, the trendy shops are centred around the 'Golden Triangle' of place des Grands Hommes, allées de Tourny and cours George Clémenceau. Recently smartened-up cours du Chapeau Rouge and cours de l'Intendance are chic, pedestrianised streets, with **Hermès** (ⓐ 2 pl. Gambetta ⓣ (05) 56 52 41 25) and **Le Tanneur** (ⓐ 9 cours de l'Intendance ⓣ (05) 56 81 91 98 ⓦ www.letanneur.com), among many others. More high street shops and Galeries Lafayette (see page 67) are on rue Sainte Catherine, Europe's longest pedestrianised shopping street. For some interesting interiors shops, one-off boutiques and upmarket antique outlets, head over to Chartrons, the old merchant's district. Don't leave without exploring rue Faubourg des Arts, where small artisan workshops abound. Past place de la Bourse is Saint Pierre, where you'll find more antiques shops (often offering really good value). The pedestrianised Old Town is full of clothes, interiors, books and gift-shops. Many are centred around place du Parlement,

● *Shopping on rue Sainte Catherine*

USEFUL SHOPPING PHRASES

What time do the shops (this shop) open/close?
Á quelle heure ouvrent/ferment les magasins (ce magasin)?
Ah kel urr oovra/fairm leh magazahn (suh magazahn)?

Can I try this on?
Puis-je essayer ceci?
Pwee zher ehssayeh suhsee?

My size is...
Ma taille est...
Ma tie eh...

Do you take credit cards?
Prenez-vous les cartes de crédit?
Pruhnay voo leh kart der krehdee?

How much is this?
Ça fait combien?
Sa fay kombyen?

I'll take this one, thank you
Je prends celui-ci/celle-ci merci
Zher prohn selwee-see/sell-see mehrsee

place Camille Jullian and the pretty rue Pas St Georges.

Bigger shopping centres are found in Mériadeck, just north of place Gambetta and on the ring road around the city, notably at Bordeaux Lac, where you'll find everything in the **Auchan complex** (t (05) 56 43 44 00 w www.auchan.fr) from mobile phone shops to large jewellers.

Markets in Bordeaux are mainly food orientated, but there are several antique fairs held throughout the year, where you'll always have a chance of picking up a nifty bargain.

Eating & drinking

Bordeaux is a gourmet's heaven. The food is typically southwestern – duck, *foie gras* and truffles being the specialities – but there are also lighter options influenced by the proximity of the Atlantic Ocean. The coastal town of Arcachon, 50 km (31 miles) to the west of Bordeaux, farms 60 per cent of France's oysters, and stalls selling them line the streets of the Bordeaux regions of Entre deux Mers and Graves (particularly during the winter months, when oysters are at their best). A great gourmet half-day out is a trip to the oyster beds to watch farmers gathering them early in the morning. (An hour later, you can sample them.)

Back to those regional specialities: duck products are influential, especially *foie gras* (duck liver paté), *magret de canard* (duck breast) and *confit de canard* (duck rillettes). Other local meats include Bazas beef, Pauillac lamb and *grenier médocain*, a kind of spiced pork belly. The most famous local dish is an *entrecôte bordelaise* (steak), with plenty of shallots and red wine sauce.

PRICE CATEGORIES

The following guide indicates the average price per head for a two- to three-course dinner, excluding drinks. Lunch will usually be cheaper, and most restaurants offer a very good value *prix fixe* (fixed price) option between 12.00 and 14.00.

£ up to €25   **££** €26–45   **£££** over €45

USEFUL DINING PHRASES

I would like a table for ... people
Je voudrais une table pour ... personnes
Zher voodray oon tabl poor ... pehrson

Waiter/waitress
Monsieur/mademoiselle
M'syer/madmwahzel

Could I have this rare/medium/well cooked
Je le voudrais saignant/à point/bien cuit
Zher ler voodray saynyohn/ah pwan/bi-yen kwee

Can I see the wine list?
La carte des vins s'il vous plaît?
Lah kart day vahn, seel voo pleh?

I am vegetarian
Je suis végétarien/végétarienne
Zher swee vehjaytaryan/vehjaytaryanne

Where are the toilets please?
Où sont les toilettes s'il vous plaît?
Oo son leh twahlet, seel voo pleh?

May I have the bill, please?
L'addition s'il vous plaît
L'adission, seel voo pleh

Fish of all kinds are plentiful. Perhaps the most famous is Lamprey, a fanged eel that's cooked in vast quantities of red wine. The *alose*, or shad, is another native fish, best served simply, grilled in butter over *sarments* (vine cuttings).

Central Bordeaux has a number of wonderful markets. Among the best are the Sunday morning organic market on the quai des Chartrons and the Capucins market (see page 67).

Most of the bars and restaurants are centred around the pedestrianised Old Town and Chartrons, which offers plenty of

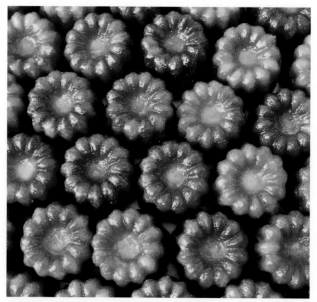

🔺 Canelés – *the small caramelised cake from Bordeaux*

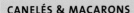

CANELÉS & MACARONS

The sweet specialities of Bordeaux have a long history. Strictly speaking, *canelés* belong to Bordeaux and *macarons* to Saint Émilion, but you'll find both of them accompanying your coffee. *Canelés* are small domed cakes made from batter, caramelised on the outside and soft and creamy on the inside (legend has it that the recipe arose from all the left-over yolks from wine production, as the whites of the eggs were used to filter the wine naturally). Macaroons (or *macarons*) have evolved from a centuries-old recipe, tiny and light made from egg whites, sugar and almonds.

Chinese, Japanese, Indian and Thai establishments to break up the French food. Increasingly the city has realised that wine bars are the way forward. If you want to experiment, the Lillet aperitif (a blend of wine and fruit liqueurs, recommended occasionally by James Bond, incidentally) also comes from Bordeaux.

Bordeaux conforms to the national opening hours – you need to eat lunch between 12.00 and 14.00, at which hour restaurants largely close until around 19.00, with last orders around 22.00.

At almost all restaurants you will be given a *pichet d'eau* when you sit down, a jug of tap water that is perfectly safe to drink.

As is usual in France, a 15 per cent service charge is included in the bill in restaurants, although often not in cafés. It is often customary to add another two to three per cent on top if the service has been good.

Entertainment & nightlife

The good news is that Bordeaux's nocturnal entertainments scene is exploding; the bad news is that the pitiless, survival-of-the-grooviest law of nature means that many of the smaller clubs open up and close down on a regular basis – so it's always worth phoning ahead to check before going.

The recent proliferation of wine bars has been a most welcome phenomenon, and not just because it's put the wine-

luvvies' noses out of joint; try CIVB Wine Bar (see page 13),
Le Petit Bois (ⓐ rue du Chai des Farines ⓣ (05) 56 79 06 46)
and Le Wine Bar (see page 71). The main English pubs are found
in Chartrons, such as The Cambridge Arms (see page 87) or near
cours Victor Hugo, where the **Frog and Rosbif** (ⓐ 23 rue d'Ausone
ⓣ (05) 56 48 55 85) has big video screens to show sporting
events. Irish pubs aren't exactly thin on the ground either – the
most lively being Molly Malone's (see page 87) and the surreally

ⓥ *Entertainment spots abound near the place de la Bourse*

named **O'Rowlands** (@ 50 rue de Pessac ✆ (05) 56 99 18 76). For the student bars whose patrons are doing their best to replace the city's wine culture with one built around beer, head to place de la Victoire and the surrounding roads. Bordeaux's best known gay bar is **Bar de l'Hôtel de Ville** (@ BHV, 4 rue de l'Hôtel de Ville ✆ (05) 56 44 05 08).

The more chic bars are found around the Grand Théâtre, the quays around place de la Bourse and Chartrons, and the Triangle d'Or – often a good place to start out an evening. At the far end of quai Bacalan, the Bassins à Flot have a few good nightclubs and a very chic restaurant, La Dame de Shanghai (see page 86), which has a bar and DJ downstairs at weekends. Around Hangar 14 on the quays, lots of new bars and restaurants have opened up recently. Its nightlife scene will be helped enormously now the new tram line has opened up along this top section of the quays. This is definitely an area to watch.

For the later part of your evening, the quai de Paludate is your best bet as most of the clubs, bars and live music venues are around here, from the cavernous **La Distillerie** (@ 96 quai de Paludate ✆ (05) 56 49 59 49) at the far end of the strip to the ever-popular **Shadow Lounge** (@ 5 rue Cabanac). For a more unusual evening, there's always **Macunaima** (@ 31 av. du Dr Schinazi, north of rue Achard ✆ (05) 56 39 97 05 🌐 www.macunaima.org), a Brazilian cultural centre offering salsa classes, regular concerts, and even an annual mini carnival.

For live music and great atmosphere, try **Comptoir du Jazz** (@ 59 quai de Paludate ✆ (05) 56 49 29 12). Other key live music venues include **Rock School Barbey** (@ 18 cours Barbey ✆ (05) 56 33 66 00 🌐 www.rockschool-barbey.com), which,

🔺 *Bordeaux's Grand Théâtre*

if it could be built out of denim, would be.

There's a casino at Bordeaux Lac (ⓐ rue Cardinal Richaud
ⓣ (05) 56 69 49 00), but don't expect Las Vegas. There are plenty of
cinemas. For films in *version originale* (look for VO after the title of
the film), head for **Utopia** (ⓐ 5 pl. Camille Jullian ⓣ (05) 56 52 00 03
ⓦ www.cinemas-utopia.org/bordeaux) or **UGC Georges Bonnac**
(ⓐ 13–15 rue Georges Bonnac ⓣ 08 92 89 28 92).

Local listings publications include *Spirit* and *Club et Concerts*,
both of which are free monthly publications, available widely
in bars and cafés, and often at the tourist office.

Sport & relaxation

The many parks and quays along the Garonne offer plenty of fresh air potential, and the city's location close to the ocean means there are also plenty of watersports.

SPECTATOR SPORTS

Equestrianism Several large jumping events are held around Bordeaux, especially in Arcachon and Bordeaux Lac. **Jumping International** (ⓦ www.bordeaux-expo.com/jumping) is the largest, held at Bordeaux Lac in the first week of February.

The **Hippodrome de Bordeaux** (ⓐ av. d'Eysines, Le Bouscat ⓣ (05) 56 28 06 74 ⓦ www.hippodromebordeauxlebouscat.com), a reopened track in the smart suburb of Le Bouscat, is a great venue for watching horse racing.

🔺 *Enjoy horse racing at the Hippodrome*

Football Bordeaux's football club is the **FC Girondins** (ⓐ Stade Chaban-Delmas ⓣ 08 92 68 34 33 ⓦ www.girondins.com). Their supporters are both vocal and loyal, making any match attendance enormous fun.

Rugby Rugby is a religion in the southwest of France. The local outfit, **USB-CABBG** (ⓐ 25 rue Delphin Loche ⓣ (05) 57 35 99 99 ⓦ www.rugby33.com), was formed in 2006 and plays home matches at the Stade André Moga in Bègles.

PARTICIPATION SPORTS

Association AIR Rollerblading around the city and skating along the quai des Chartrons are both organised by this excellent group. ⓣ (05) 56 81 21 44 ⓦ www.assoair.com

Centre de Voile This is the best sailing and windsurfing centre in Bordeaux Lac. ⓐ Boulevard du Parc des Expositions, Bruges ⓣ (05) 57 10 60 35 ⓦ www.voilebordeaux-lac.fr.st

RELAXATION

Piscine Judaïque A large public swimming pool with a gorgeous art deco interior and a retractable roof which is opened in summer. ⓐ 166 rue Judaïque ⓣ (05) 56 51 48 31 ⓛ 12.00–14.00, 16.30–19.00 Tues, Fri, 10.00–18.00 Wed, 12.00–14.00, 16.30–21.00 Thur, 12.00–18.00 Sat, 09.00–13.00, 15.00–18.00 Sun

Sources de Caudalie A wine spa – yes, a wine spa – set among the vines of Château Smith Haut Lafitte. Try a Cabernet scrub, a Sauvignon massage, or a jacuzzi in a wine barrel (but mind the splinters). ⓐ Chemin de Smith Haut Lafitte, Bordeaux-Martillac ⓣ (05) 57 83 83 83 ⓦ www.sources-caudalie.com

Accommodation

Accommodation in Bordeaux can be lacking in high season or during popular festivals, so book well in advance. It's also worth checking out *chambres d'hôtes* (guest houses) and the various châteaux on the outskirts of the city. Note that breakfast is not always included in the room rate.

Auberge de Jeunesse Barbey £ Cheap and cheerful, with kitchen and internet access. Groups need to book one month in advance. ⓐ 20 cours Barbey (The Old Town, Saint Pierre & Saint Michel) ⓣ (05) 56 33 00 70 ⓦ www.auberge-jeunesse-bordeaux.com ⓝ Tram: Victoire

Hôtel du Parc £ Eight bedrooms, and very simple, but well priced and two minutes from the Jardin Public. ⓐ 10 rue de la Verrerie (Golden Triangle, Jardin Public, Chartrons & Bacalan) ⓣ (05) 56 52 78 20 ⓝ Tram: Jardin Public

Eco Lodge de Chartrons ££ Hidden away on a side street just next to the renovated Bordeaux quays, this is a small and friendly hotel

PRICE CATEGORIES

The price given is the average for one double room, for one night. Some rates vary during the busy summer months, but Bordeaux doesn't alter its rates too much in high season.
£ up to €50 **££** €50–100 **£££** over €100

with a large sitting room and well-designed rooms. ⓐ 23 rue
Raze (Golden Triangle, Jardin Public, Chartrons & Bacalan)
ⓣ (05) 56 81 49 13 ⓦ www.ecolodgedeschartrons.com
Ⓝ Tram: Chartrons

Hôtel de Normandie ££ Simple, clean and very smart. Located right
next to the École du Vin wine school. ⓐ 7 cours du 30 juillet (Golden
Triangle, Jardin Public, Chartrons & Bacalan) ⓣ (05) 56 52 16 80
ⓦ www.hotel-de-normandie-bordeaux.com Ⓝ Tram: Grand Théâtre

Hôtel Notre Dame ££ Simple, well-located hotel, just by
the main square in Chartrons. Small bar downstairs. ⓐ 36 rue
Notre-Dame (Golden Triangle, Jardin Public, Chartrons & Bacalan)
ⓣ (05) 56 52 88 24 ⓦ www.hotelnotredame.free.fr Ⓝ Tram: Place
Paul Doumer

Hôtel des Quatre Soeurs ££ Well located right by the Grand
Théâtre, unexceptional (although there are a few large, art
deco rooms) but very popular. ⓐ 6 cours du 30 juillet (Golden
Triangle, Jardin Public, Chartrons & Bacalan) ⓣ (05) 57 81 19 20
ⓦ www.hotel-bordeaux-centre.com Ⓝ Tram: Grand Théâtre

Hôtel Restaurant Le Gambetta ££ Right by the pretty Porte Dijeaux,
this is great for exploring the pedestrianised Old Town. ⓐ 66 rue
de la Porte Dijeaux (The Old Town, Saint Pierre & Saint Michel)
ⓣ (05) 56 51 21 83 ⓦ www.hotel-gambetta.com Ⓝ Tram: Gambetta

Une Chambre en Ville £££ Chic, beautifully decorated B&B in the
Old Town serving great breakfasts. Only five rooms, so book ahead.

ⓐ 35 rue Bouffard (The Old Town, Saint Pierre & Saint Michel)
ⓣ (05) 56 81 34 53 ⓦ www.bandb-bx.com ⓝ Tram: Gambetta

Château Grattequina £££ You get to live out the château fantasy in this 19th-century building overlooking the Garonne River in Bacalan. ⓐ av. de Labarde, Blanquefort (The Right Bank, Bordeaux Lac, Bouliac & beyond) ⓣ (05) 56 35 76 76
ⓦ www.grattequina.com

Golf du Médoc Hôtel & Spa £££ Newly opened golf hotel, where you can walk out onto the fairway. Twenty minutes' drive from central Bordeaux. ⓐ chemin de Courmateau, Le Pian Médoc-Louens (The Right Bank, Bordeaux Lac, Bouliac & beyond)
ⓣ (05) 56 70 31 31 ⓦ www.hotelgolfdumedoc.com

Hauterive Saint-James £££ Designed by Jean Nouvel, this swish hotel offers Michelin-starred food. ⓐ 3 pl. Camille Hostein, Bouliac (The Right Bank, Bordeaux Lac, Bouliac & beyond)
ⓣ (05) 57 97 06 00 ⓦ www.saintjames-bouliac.com ⓝ Bus: 7

Hôtel Burdigala £££ 5-star hotel near the Mériadeck shopping centre, with a swimming pool. ⓐ 115 rue Georges-Bonnac (The Old Town, Saint Pierre & Saint Michel) ⓣ (05) 56 90 16 16
ⓦ www.burdigala.com ⓝ Tram: Gambetta or Mériadeck

Maison Bord'eaux £££ A city-centre boutique hotel that's a great base for vineyard visitors. ⓐ 113 rue du Docteur Albert Barraud (Golden Triangle, Jardin Public, Chartrons & Bacalan) ⓣ (05) 56 44 00 45
ⓦ www.lamaisonbordeaux.com ⓝ Bus: 53, 54, 55

The Regent Bordeaux £££ Luxurious finishes on every room, a roof spa, three restaurants and a ballroom make this *the* place to stay. ⓐ 2 pl. de la Comédie (Golden Triangle, Jardin Public, Chartrons & Bacalan) ⓣ (05) 57 30 44 44 ⓦ www.theregentbordeaux.com ⓝ Tram: Grand Théâtre

Seekoo Hôtel £££ Niftily designed and sparkling white, this hotel is the smart choice for a city-centre billet. ⓐ 54 quai Bacalan (Golden Triangle, Jardin Public, Chartrons & Bacalan) ⓣ (05) 56 39 07 07 ⓦ www.seekoo-hotel.com ⓝ Tram: Chartrons or Les Hangars

Sources de Caudalie £££ Sumptious, faux-rustic styling and Chardonnay facials. Two fab restaurants and great views. ⓐ Chemin de Smith Haut Lafitte, Bordeaux-Martillac (The Right Bank, Bordeaux Lac, Bouliac & beyond) ⓣ (05) 57 83 83 83 ⓦ www.sources-caudalie.com

🔺 *La Grange au Bateau rooms at Sources de Caudalie*

THE BEST OF BORDEAUX

Whether you're a wine lover, a history buff or a surfer, Bordeaux and its regions offer plenty of tempting options.

TOP 10 ATTRACTIONS

- **Grand Théâtre** Impressive on the outside, gorgeous on the inside; make sure you get cultural in style while you're here (see page 81)

- **The vineyards of Saint Émilion** You can't come to Bordeaux without at least eyeballing a few vines (see page 116)

- **Cathédrale Saint-André & Tour Pey-Berland** Ogle at the 14th-century, double-whammy Gothic wonder of the cathedral and the adjacent bell tower (see page 56)

- **Cuisine** Make the most of the many restaurants around the pedestrianised place du Parlement or the wide stretches of the quai des Chartrons (see Eating & drinking, page 24)

🔻 *The rose window of Cathédrale Saint-André*

- **CAPC Musée d'Art Contemporain (Museum of Contemporary Art)** An art museum that almost vibrates with the energy of its exhibits (see page 80)

- **Quayside architecture** Stroll past the 18th-century buildings that span out on either side from place des Quinconces (see page 79)

- **Jardin Public** The city's most beautiful public park, with botanical gardens, a café, boat trips around the lake and a museum of natural history (see page 77)

- **Base Sous-Marine** What would you do with a disused U-boat pen? The Bordelais converted theirs into an art space (see page 79)

- **The beaches of Arcachon & the Atlantic Coast** Don't miss chic Cap Ferret and Europe's highest sand dune at the Dune de Pyla (see page 104)

- **The Miroir d'Eau** A reflective water feature opposite the Bourse has turned into a giant paddling pool (see page 61)

Suggested itineraries

HALF-DAY: BORDEAUX IN A HURRY

In summer, take the tram along the quays to place de la Bourse and enjoy the Miroir d'Eau water feature (see page 61). Take a stroll along the quai des Chartrons , where you can eat at one of the many pavement cafés. In winter, substitute the Miroir d'Eau for a trip to the CAPC Museum of Contemporary Art (see page 80).

1 DAY: TIME TO SEE A LITTLE MORE

Once you've done the above, make Cathédrale Saint-André and Tour Pey-Berland (see page 56) your priority – so close that they share an address, the former offers stunning stained glass, the latter fab views. Now you're in the Old Town, spend the afternoon taking in the Centre Jean Moulin (see page 64) to learn about the astonishing exploits of the region's Resistance. Have a rest-those-legs evening and indulge yourself by dining at one of the city's best restaurants, followed by an opera at the Grand Théâtre (see page 81).

2–3 DAYS: TIME TO SEE MUCH MORE

Explore the quays, going right up to the Cap Sciences and the Bassins à Flot. Then visit a *négociant* (wine merchant) that's open to the public and find out a bit more about the infinite subject of wine. Alternatively, get stuck into some shopping with an afternoon in the chic boutiques around the place des Grands Hommes and cours du Chapeau Rouge. In the evening, eat at a restaurant on the allées de Tourny.

LONGER: ENJOYING BORDEAUX TO THE FULL

If you have an extra day, make sure you explore the surrounding countryside and coast. Hire a car or take a train out to Saint Émilion for some vineyard exploration or to Arcachon and the Dune de Pyla for a walk on the beach. Or take a boat taxi down the Garonne.

⬥ *Pey-Berland: one of the first stops on any Bordeaux itinerary*

Something for nothing

Bordeaux has over 300 UNESCO World Heritage Sites and monuments to explore, almost all of them free, as well as over 20 parks and gardens and the wide sweep of the Garonne River with a 4 km (2½ mile) pathway running along either side. This means there is more than enough open space for wandering around that won't cost you a thing. Among the many parks, the Jardin Public (see page 77) and Parc Bordelais (see page 78) are especially good for children, with Punch and Judy shows and pony rides in summer. For people-watching, try the Skate Park on quai des Chartrons (see page 79) or the Miroir d'Eau and surrounding Jardin des Lumières (see page 61) along the river front. The Jardin Botanique (see page 93) over on the Right Bank is another lovely park for wandering around, with its Zen-like water features.

On the first Sunday of every month, art galleries are free. The city centre is also closed to cars on the same day, and there are often small street markets and a variety of entertainments laid on. Many museums are in fact free throughout the month, including the Musée d'Aquitaine (see page 64) and the Musée des Beaux-Arts (see page 65). But do note that temporary exhibitions almost always have a charge.

Among the many examples of fine 18th-century architecture, seek out Jacques Gabriel's allées de Tourny (see page 72), Victor Louis' Grand Théâtre (see page 81) and Richard Rogers' Tribunal de Grand Instance (see page 62). In Quartier Saint Eloi, at the end of cours de l'Intendance, you can see Montaigne's old house at 23–25 rue de la Rousselle.

🔺 *Relax and meander through one of Bordeaux's many parks*

The markets are all free entry, and certainly make for a fascinating couple of people-watching, bargain-spotting hours; you don't have to buy anything. The best outdoor ones are in Saint Pierre and Saint Michel on weekend mornings.

When it rains

Bordeaux's location just inland from the Atlantic Ocean means it is no stranger to rainy days. One of the best things to do is to get out into the vineyards and visit a few properties – among the best for non wine specialists is La Winery (see page 97).

The many beautiful churches that are dotted throughout the city centre will provide some spectacular environments in which to shelter and, indeed, totally forget about such trifles as the weather. The basilicas of **Saint-Michel** (② pl. Duborg), and Saint-Seurin (see page 72) are UNESCO World Heritage Sites, and Église Saint-Louis des Chartrons (see page 76) has free concert recitals on Sunday afternoons. The city's main cathedral, Cathédrale Saint-André (see page 56), has stunning stained-glass windows.

Alternatively, get a culture fix at a museum – you can look at the archaeological heritage of the area at the Musée d'Aquitaine (see page 64), indulge in some art gazing at the Musée des Beaux-Arts (see page 65), or go avant-garde at the CAPC Museum of Contemporary Art (see page 80).

No rainy day is complete without some shopping – what a great excuse. Pas St Georges's books and clothes shops constitute a legitimate alternative to the frizzies, as does the array of stores at Mériadeck indoor shopping centre (see page 66), which also has plenty of cafés and fast food outlets. Once you're all shopped out, head to Cinéma Utopia (see page 31) to catch an English-language film.

You could also embrace the rain by going to the Miroir d'Eau (see page 61) to really splash in puddles, or take a swim at the Piscine Judaïque (see page 33).

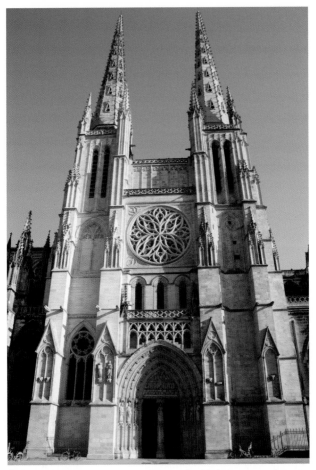

🔺 Bordeaux's cathedral provides a captivating (and dry) glimpse into the past

On arrival

TIME DIFFERENCE

Bordeaux is on Central European Time (GMT +1). Clocks go forward one hour between end March and end October for Daylight Saving.

ARRIVING

By air

Bordeaux-Mérignac international airport (☏ (05) 56 34 50 50 ⓦ www.bordeaux.aeroport.fr) is situated around 10 km (6 miles) outside the city. The most convenient way to reach your accommodation is by taxi. The taxi rank is situated on the arrivals level of Hall B, or you can book one in advance from **Taxi Mérignac** (☏ (05) 56 97 11 27). A journey to the city centre should cost around €30–45.

A bus connects the airport to Gare Saint-Jean (see below), leaving every 45 minutes from Terminal B, 07.45–22.45. The return service departs from 06.45–21.45. Tickets are €7, phone ☏ (05) 56 34 50 50 for details.

By rail

The main TGV train station in Bordeaux is **Gare Saint-Jean** (ⓐ rue Charles Domercq ☏ 3635 (within France) ⓦ www.voyages-sncf.com), which is about 4 km (just over 2 miles) outside the city centre, on the Left Bank of the Garonne River. Trains arrive from all over France, including at least six a day from Paris. The tram line that goes to place des Quinconces in central Bordeaux starts directly outside, and the tourist office is opposite the tram stop at Quinconces.

By road

The bus station is in the city centre, at the **Hatte Routière terminal** (ⓐ allées de Chartres), where most of the buses into and around Bordeaux start and stop. Most buses are run by Trans'Gironde.

Access by car comes from Paris on the A10, and up from Toulouse on the A62, and from Arcachon, Biarritz and Spain on the A63. For traffic information when you travel, phone **Traffic info** ❶ 08 05 90 33 33.

The many underground car parks give excellent access to the main shopping areas. Expect to spend €10–15 for a full day's parking.

⬤ *The main station in Bordeaux – Gare Saint-Jean*

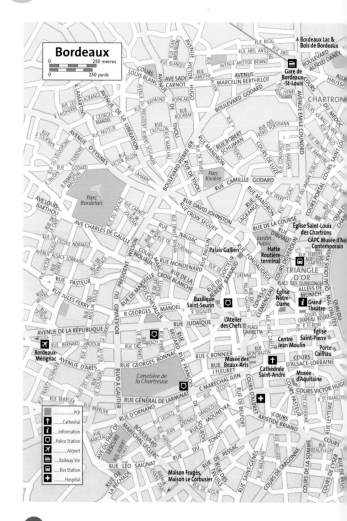

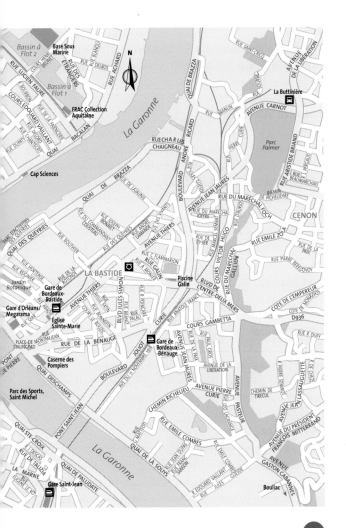

By water

The nearest international passenger ferry ports are at Caen up in northern France, or Santander down in Spain, from where travel would have to be by road or rail.

FINDING YOUR FEET

Bordeaux is a safe city by pretty much any standard. You might want to be careful around the train station and quai de Paludate or quai Bacalan at night, but other than that, the usual warnings about pickpockets and traffic apply.

There are some great tours offered by the Office de Tourisme. The UNESCO Tour runs by bus at night a few times a week during the summer and visits the key monuments. There are also guided walks, bike tours, horse-drawn carriage tours, architecture tours and gourmet tours. If you're visiting several sights, the 'Bordeaux Pass' gives access to various attractions. Details are available from the tourist office (see page 134).

ORIENTATION

Bordeaux is divided in two by the Garonne River. The easiest way to get your bearings is to work out where the river is – and thus place des Quinconces, the largest square in the city that divides the Old Town from Chartrons and Bacalan.

GETTING AROUND

Trams and buses provide an easy, cheap way of getting around Bordeaux. The trams (sometimes called 'metro' by locals) are modern, clean and very attractive. Make sure that you buy a ticket in advance and validate it on board. A single trip costs €1.40, or

IF YOU GET LOST, TRY...

Sorry to bother you, but...
Excusez-moi de vous déranger, mais...
Ekskezay-mwah der voo dayronjay, may...

Could you tell me the way to...
Comment fait-on pour aller à ...
Kohmohn feyt-ohn poor al-lay ah ...

Do you speak English?
Parlez-vous anglais?
Pahrlay-voo ahnglay?

Could you point to it on my map?
Pouvez-vous me le montrer sur la carte?
Poo vay voo muh ler montray soor lah kart?

you can buy better value passes which allow five or ten trips or unlimited travel for one or seven days. Single tickets allow you to change trams within one hour of validation. Bus routes also criss-cross the city, using the same ticket system as trams.

Trams and buses are run by **Réseau Connex** (☎ (05) 57 57 88 88 🌐 www.infotbc.com).

There are three tram lines – A, B and C – running through the city. A fourth, line D in the north of the city, is planned for completion in 2015.

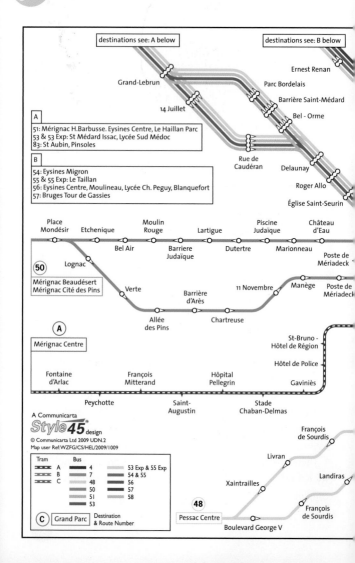

destinations see: A below

destinations see: B below

Ernest Renan

Grand-Lebrun

Parc Bordelais

Barrière Saint-Médard

14 Juillet

Bel - Orme

A

51: Mérignac H.Barbusse. Eysines Centre, Le Haillan Parc
53 & 53 Exp: St Médard Issac, Lycée Sud Médoc
83: St Aubin, Pinsoles

B

54: Eysines Migron
55 & 55 Exp: Le Taillan
56: Eysines Centre, Moulineau, Lycée Ch. Peguy, Blanquefort
57: Bruges Tour de Gassies

Rue de
Caudéran

Delaunay

Roger Allo

Église Saint-Seurin

Place
Mondésir   Etchenique

Moulin
Rouge   Lartigue

Piscine
Judaïque

Château
d'Eau

Bel Air

Barrière
Judaïque

Dutertre

Marionneau

Poste de
Mériadeck

50   Lognac

Mérignac Beaudésert
Mérignac Cité des Pins   Verte

11 Novembre   Manège

Poste de
Mériadeck

Barrière
d'Arès

A

Allée
des Pins   Chartreuse

St-Bruno -
Hôtel de Région

Mérignac Centre

Hôtel de Police

Fontaine
d'Arlac

François
Mitterand

Hôpital
Pellegrin

Gaviniès

Peychotte

Saint-
Augustin

Stade
Chaban-Delmas

A Communicarta
Style**45** design
© Communicarta Ltd 2009 UDN.2
Map user Ref:WZFG/CS/HEL/2009/1009

François
de Sourdis

Tram	Bus	
A	4	53 Exp & 55 Exp
B	7	54 & 55
C	48	56
	50	57
	51	58
	53	

Livran

Landiras

Xaintrailles

C Grand Parc   Destination
& Route Number

48   Pessac Centre

François
de Sourdis

Boulevard George V

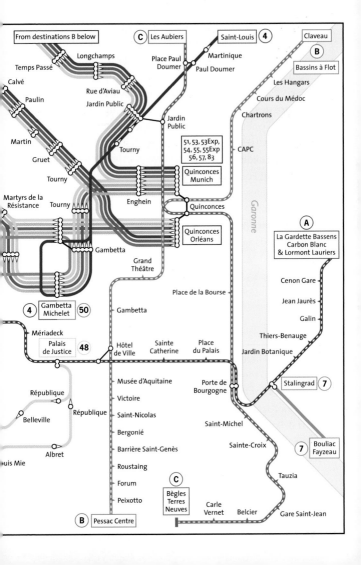

Line A runs east from the Mérignac Centre over the river towards La Gardette Bassens and Carbon Blanc in the northeast of the city. This line is the most useful for tourists as it goes through the centre of Bordeaux. Line B runs from Pessac Centre up to Claveau via the Bassins à Flot, travelling along the quai des Chartrons and past place de la Victoire. There is an interchange with line A at Hôtel de Ville and with line C at Quinconces. Line C runs from Les Aubiers to Bègles Terres Neuves via Gare Saint-Jean, passing through the Jardin Public and Saint-Michel. There is an interchange with line A at Port de Bourgogne.

Bordeaux has a number of taxi firms, including:

Allô Bordeaux ❶ (05) 56 31 61 07

Aquitaine Cars ❶ (05) 56 86 80 30

Water taxis are a special – if expensive! – way of getting around between mid-March and the end of October. The Clapotine taxi boat, run by **Évolution Garonne** (❶ (06) 07 19 75 86 ⓦ www.evolutiongaronne.com), leaves from quai des Queyries.

CAR HIRE

The main car hire companies are found at the train station and the airport. There are a few cheaper companies on the roads leading up to the station, but the big guys are all directly outside.

Europcar ❶ Bordeaux-Mérignac Airport (05) 56 34 05 79; Gare Saint-Jean 08 25 00 42 46 ⓦ www.europcar.fr

Hertz ❶ Bordeaux-Mérignac Airport (05) 56 34 59 87; Gare Saint-Jean (05) 57 59 05 95 ⓦ www.hertz.fr

Sixt ❶ Bordeaux-Mérignac Airport (05) 56 34 08 15 ⓦ www.sixt.fr

---

▶ *The Romanesque Three Graces fountain on place de la Bourse*

THE CITY OF
Bordeaux

The Old Town, Saint Pierre & Saint Michel

This is the historical heart of Bordeaux, where the pedestrianised Old Town meets cobbled squares and tiny streets filled with churches and market places, next to modern bars and student hang-outs. The majority of the UNESCO World Heritage monuments are crowded into these streets, and much of the recent renovation work has been concentrated here.

SIGHTS & ATTRACTIONS

L'Atelier des Chefs

Here you'll find cultural instruction in the form of Bordeaux-style cooking classes where you get to enjoy the finished product over a glass of wine. There's also a great shop selling cookery books and accessories. ⓐ 25 rue Judaïque ⓣ (05) 56 00 72 70 ⓦ www.atelierdeschefs.com ⓛ 10.00–19.00 ⓝ Tram: Gambetta

Cathédrale Saint-André & Tour Pey-Berland (Saint André Cathedral & Pey Berland Tower)

A 13th-century cathedral that's been half renovated, giving a stripe of clean limestone surrounded by darker, dirtier stone. The stunning interior has excellent stained-glass windows. Alongside it is the Tour Pey-Berland, a bell tower that's also open to the public. ⓐ pl. Pey-Berland ⓣ (05) 56 87 17 18 ⓛ 10.00–18.00 June–Sept; 10.00–12.00, 14.00–17.00 Oct–May; guided tours 14.00–18.00 Wed, Sat & Sun ⓝ Tram: Hôtel de Ville

◗ *The gothic allure of the Grosse Cloche*

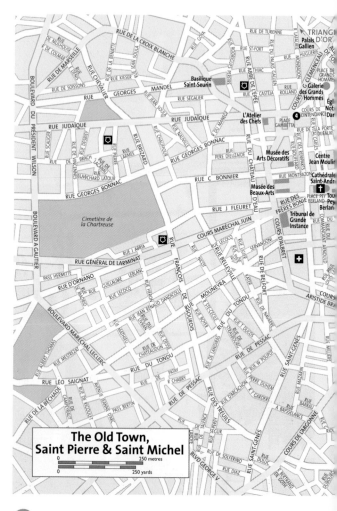

The Old Town,
Saint Pierre & Saint Michel

0 — 250 metres
0 — 250 yards

Église Saint-Pierre (Saint Pierre Church)

An imposing, Gothic-looking structure that dates from the
15th century and has additions from the 19th. ⓐ pl. Saint-Pierre
ⓘ (05) 56 94 30 50 ⓛ 09.00–18.00; guided tours 14.30–17.00
Thur ⓝ Tram: Place de la Bourse

Porte de Saint-Eloi & La Grosse Cloche (Saint Eloi Gate & The Great Bell)

The Saint Eloi gate, one of the city's old entrances, looks almost
Austrian in style, with its clock and giant bell. Today, it leads to
the chic shops of rue Saint James. ⓐ rue Saint James ⓝ Tram:
Porte de Bourgogne

Millésima

This central wine merchant's warehouse is the place to learn
all about the city's all-pervasive wine culture. There's a wine
school available, and tours offering an insight into the Bordeaux
system of selling through wine merchants. There are also over
two million bottles in the cellar and a stylish shop where you
can kit yourself out as an oenologist. ⓐ 87 quai de Paludate
ⓘ (05) 57 80 88 08 ⓦ www.millesima.fr ⓛ Appointment essential
ⓝ Tram: Sainte-Croix. Admission charge for tours & tastings

Parc des Sports, Saint Michel

At the far end of the quays, right at the entrance to the city centre,
this excellent area has a large expanse of green park together
with a beach volleyball court, a tennis wall, a children's play area,
and an urban (tarmac) football pitch. ⓐ Quai Ste-Croix ⓛ 24 hrs
ⓝ Tram: Saint-Michel or Sainte-Croix

ÉCHOPPES

As you walk around the residential parts of Saint Pierre, Saint Eloi and the Old Town, it's hard to miss the low-lying stone houses that line the streets, opening straight onto the pavement with no front garden. This is the typical Bordeaux house, and is called an *échoppe*. These are usually one-storey, low, wide stone buildings that were originally built between the 15th and 18th century as workers' and artisans' housing, but are now considered very chic, and are often beautifully restored. The architecture is very similar for all *échoppes* – usually with a walled town garden at the back, no garden at the front, a large, elaborately carved wooden front door and a symmetrical layout inside, where you have two identical living rooms on either side of a rising central stair looking out onto the road, then the kitchen and living quarters at the back, opening onto the quieter garden. Some of the best examples in Bordeaux are found in Sacré Coeur (off rue de l'École Normale), Nansouty, Saint Augustin (off allée des Pins), Camille Godard and Talence.

Place de la Bourse & the Miroir d'Eau

Fresh from renovations and one of the best urban regeneration projects in the city, the Miroir d'Eau is a huge, shallow water feature that reflects the classic 18th-century buildings and smart central fountain of the place de la Bourse. The water alternates between spray, jets and a shallow pool, and on sunny days seems to attract half the children of the city.

The flowerbeds of the Jardin des Lumières surround it on either side. pl. de la Bourse Tram: Place de la Bourse

Place Camille Jullian

Another lively pedestrianised square in the centre of the Old Town, full of cafés and bars, but also the Utopia cinema (see page 31), the best art-house cinema in Bordeaux. Tram: Place de la Bourse

Place du Parlement

The fountain at the centre of this pedestrianised square is surrounded by children playing all summer. There are restaurants stuffed into almost every corner, interspersed with the odd bookshop or clothes shop, and beautiful 18th-century houses. Tram: Place de la Bourse

Porte Cailhau

This elaborately carved stone gate was built in 1495, and marks the entrance along the quays to the Saint Pierre district. You can even explore inside it. pl. du Palais 14.00–19.00 June–Sept Tram: Porte de Bourgogne

Tribunal de Grand Instance (High Court)

Designed by Richard Rogers in 1998, this glass-and-stainless-steel creation proves that Bordeaux's architectural golden age didn't end in the 18th century. It is a working court, so while you can generally pop into the hall to have a look around you cannot enter the actual courtrooms where judging takes place. rue des Frères Bonie Tram: Hôtel de Ville

Bordeaux is any wine lover's dream destination

CULTURE

Centre Jean Moulin

The museum of the Resistance movement was set up to give a balanced view. Thus the deportation of the Jews and other dark episodes from World War II are illustrated alongside the heroics performed by the Free French Forces. ❸ 48 pl. Jean Moulin, rue Vital Carles ❶ (05) 56 79 66 00 ❷ 14.00–18.00 Tues–Sun ❷ Tram: Hôtel de Ville

Galerie Cortex Athletico (Cortex Athletico Gallery)

A large area given over to two sections, one offering workshop space to visiting artists, the other dedicated to permanent exhibitions. ❸ 1 rue des Étables ❶ (05) 56 94 31 89 ❿ www.cortexathletico.com ❷ 14.00–20.00 Thur–Sat ❷ Tram: Sainte-Croix

Musée d'Aquitaine (Museum of Aquitaine)

A museum that takes an extensive look at the archaeology and history of the region and the cultural influences that have shaped modern-day Bordeaux. There are recreations of Roman mosaic floors as well as a permanent exhibition exploring France's role in the slave trade. ❸ 20 cours Pasteur ❶ (05) 56 01 51 00 ❷ 11.00–18.00 Tues–Sun ❷ Tram: Musée d'Aquitaine

Musée des Arts Décoratifs (Museum of Decorative Arts)

A lovely cobbled courtyard marks the entrance to this small, elegant museum, displaying collections of jewellery, glassware and paintings. ❸ 39 rue Bouffard ❶ (05) 56 10 14 00 ❷ 14.00–18.00 Wed–Mon ❷ Tram: Sainte Catherine

Musée des Beaux-Arts (Museum of Fine Arts)

One of the most impressive buildings of all the city's museums, this 16th-century structure lies in the middle of the gardens of the Hôtel de Ville. Permanent and temporary exhibitions, split over two galleries, include works by Rubens and Titian, alongside those by more modern artists such as Picasso and Dufy. ⓐ 20 cours d'Albret ⓣ (05) 56 96 61 50 ⓛ 11.00–18.00 Wed–Mon ⓝ Tram: Hôtel de Ville

Musée National des Douanes (National Customs Museum)

By place de la Bourse, this former tax office for passing shipping trade is now a museum looking at the history of that area of commerce in the region. ⓐ 1 pl. de la Bourse ⓣ (05) 56 48 82 82 ⓛ 10.00–18.00 Tues–Sun ⓝ Tram: Place de la Bourse

RETAIL THERAPY

Bordeaux's Old Town is full of small, interesting shops in which to spend a few (dozen) hours. As you would expect, there is a high density of wine shops, most of which offer shipping overseas. Running between place du Parlement and place Camille Jullian, rue du Pas St Georges is a treasure trove of clothes shops, card shops, hairdressers, bookshops, newsagents, cafés and interior design places. The smart street of rue Bouffard is known for its antique stores, and also has some good interior design shops.

Bayonne Chocolate Delicious chocolates made from a town around two hours south of Bordeaux, approaching the Spanish border. The signature is a dark, spicy chocolate. ⓐ 6 rue des Remparts

ⓣ (05) 56 44 55 72 ⓛ 09.30–18.00 Mon–Sat ⓝ Tram: Sainte Catherine; bus: 4

Centre Mériadeck Large and central shopping centre, with a supermarket and also a range of smaller, more interesting shops. ⓐ rue du Château d'Eau ⓣ (05) 56 93 00 15 ⓛ 09.30–20.00 Mon–Sat, 10.30–16.00 Sun ⓝ Tram: Mériadeck

Cousin & Compagnie A friendly, well-designed wine shop stocking bottles from Spain, Italy and further afield, as well as well-chosen boutique wines from around Bordeaux. Knowledgeable, often English-speaking staff and regular tasting evenings. ⓐ 2 rue de Pas St Georges ⓣ (05) 56 01 20 23 ⓦ www.cousin.fr ⓛ 16.00–22.00 Mon–Sat, 14.00–20.00 Sun ⓝ Tram: Place de la Bourse

⬤ *Bordeaux's food markets are among the finest in Europe*

MARKETS

If you like your fodder fresh, an early-start trip to Capucins market will be just the job. This is the place where the local restaurants buy their food, and, when you've bought yours, grab an early brunch at the delicious oyster bar. ⓐ pl. des Capucins ⓛ 06.00–13.00 Tues–Sun ⓝ Tram: Sainte-Croix

Antiques lovers will enjoy a jaunt to Passage Saint Michel, a charming antiques centre in which around 40 dealers display their wares. There are often bric-à-brac and antique stalls laid out on the square in front of the Saint-Michel basilica as well. ⓐ 14–17 pl. Canteloup ⓣ (05) 56 92 14 76 ⓛ 09.30–18.30 Mon–Sat, 08.00–14.00 Sun ⓝ Tram: Porte de Bourgogne

Galeries Lafayette France's signature department store has two buildings in this part of Bordeaux: the main store at no. 11 has clothes and accessories for women as well as a good café on the third floor, while just opposite is the men's store. ⓐ 11 rue Sainte Catherine ⓣ (05) 56 44 46 59 ⓦ www.galerieslafayette.com ⓛ 10.00–19.00 Mon–Sat ⓝ Tram: Grand Théâtre

L'Oenolimit This friendly wine shop has a large selection of bottles from Bordeaux (of course), but also further afield. Wine tastings are held regularly, as are fun evenings such as oyster and white wine pairing. ⓐ 2 rue des Ayres ⓣ 335 57 88 34 19 ⓦ www.loenolimit.com ⓛ 10.00–22.00 ⓝ Tram: Port de Bourgogne

TAKING A BREAK

Karl £ ❶ One of the most relaxed and fun breakfast spots in town. Long wooden benches and large windows make this a café that you could find in Sydney or Barcelona, and there's a great range of patisseries, breads, and larger snacks. Excellent soups and salads at lunchtime. ⓐ pl. du Parlement ❶ (05) 56 81 01 00 🕒 08.30–19.30 Ⓝ Tram: Place de la Bourse

Cafés des Arts £–££ ❷ Classic French bistro fare in the student quarter with a lively bar attached. ⓐ 138 cours Victor Hugo ❶ (05) 56 91 78 46 🕒 07.30–00.00 Ⓝ Tram: Musée d'Aquitaine

Couleurs Sucrées £–££ ❸ There's a wide choice of herbal teas and sweet treats at this welcoming *salon de thé*. ⓐ 12 rue du

Ⓐ *Go to Karl for a great breakfast or lunch*

Parlement Saint-Pierre, between pl. du Parlement & pl. Saint-Pierre ① (05) 56 79 30 90 ② 10.00–21.00 Tues–Sat Ⓝ Tram: Place de la Bourse

Le Grand Café £–££ ❹ Well located, outside tables and pretty much always open – what more can you ask for? Good, bistro-style food is served for lunch and dinner, but coffees, drinks and snacks are available all day. ⓐ 65 cours de l'Intendance ① (05) 56 52 61 10 ② 07.30–01.00 Ⓝ Tram: Grand Théâtre

Le Grand Castan £–££ ❺ Perfectly located on the quays, opposite the Miroir d'Eau, this eccentric bar was opened in the 19th century and has a grotto-style back wall (they love this effect in Bordeaux for some reason) and a good range of drinks and cocktails. ⓐ 2 quai de la Douane ① (05) 56 44 51 97 ② 09.00–02.00 Ⓝ Tram: Place de la Bourse

AFTER DARK

RESTAURANTS
Le Charles Dickens ££ ❻ A smart English pub on the waterfront, offering good beers, decent meals and a wide range of sporting fixtures on a large-screen TV. ⓐ Quai de la Douane ① (05) 56 30 41 96 ② 15.00–02.00 Mon–Fri, 13.00–02.00 Sat & Sun Ⓝ Tram: Place de la Bourse

Le Gabriel ££–£££ ❼ A glamorous location for this café-bistro-restaurant, housed over three floors that ascend in terms of gastronomy as well as price. ⓐ 10 pl. de la Bourse

● *Le Grand Castan is one of the popular café bars on the quays*

① (05) 56 30 00 80 **🕐** 09.00–01.00 (restaurant: 12.00–13.30, 19.30–21.30) **🌐** www.bordeaux-gabriel.fr **Ⓜ** Tram: Place de la Bourse

Moshi Moshi ££–£££ **❽** Excellent Japanese restaurant housed in an old cellar. The downstairs toilets are worth the trip alone, with their mini Zen gardens and water dripping out of bamboo shoots. **ⓐ** 8 pl. Fernand Lafargue, between rue St-James & rue Ayre **①** (05) 56 79 22 91 **🌐** www.restaurantmoshimoshi.com **🕐** 20.00–22.30 Tues–Thur, 20.00–23.30 Fri & Sat **Ⓜ** Tram: Porte de Bourgogne

La Tupina ££–£££ **❾** One of Bordeaux's best-loved bistros, where mega-chef Jean Pierre Xaradakis presides over his open fire, cooking up chunks of meat that wouldn't be out of place on Tony Soprano's table. ⓐ 12 rue Porte de la Monnaie, between rue du Hamel & quai Sainte-Croix ⓣ (05) 56 91 56 37 ⓦ www.latupina.com ⓛ 12.00–14.00, 19.00–23.00 ⓝ Tram: Sainte-Croix

PUBS, BARS & CLUBS

Absolut Lounge Popular and lively, this place isn't the cheapest bar in Bordeaux, but it does have a good range of schnapps and cocktails. ⓐ 14 rue de la Devise ⓣ (05) 56 48 80 00 ⓛ 17.00–02.00 ⓝ Tram: Place de la Bourse

Café Brun Great atmosphere at this Irish-vibed bar, which serves some of the best Guinness in town. ⓐ 45 rue Saint-Rémi ⓣ (05) 56 52 20 49 ⓛ 09.00–02.00 Mon–Sat, 15.00–02.00 Sun ⓝ Tram: Place de la Bourse

Le Port de la Lune Live jazz, friendly staff, a good bar and a bistro next door make this a Bordeaux institution. ⓐ 58 quai de Paludate ⓣ (05) 56 49 15 55 ⓦ www.leportdelalune.com ⓛ 12.00-14.30, 19.00–02.00 (kitchen closes 01.00) ⓝ Tram: Sainte-Croix

Saintex Big music venue with regular live concerts. ⓐ 54 cours de la Marne ⓣ (05) 56 31 21 04 ⓦ http://saintex33.free.fr ⓛ 21.00–02.00 Wed–Sat ⓝ Tram: Hôtel de Ville

Le Wine Bar A good wine bar in a lively student area. It's on one of the winding (driveable) roads on the outskirts of the pedestrianised centre. ⓐ 19 rue Bahutiers ⓣ (05) 56 48 56 99 ⓦ www.lewinebar-bordeaux.com ⓛ 11.00–14.00, 18.00–23.30 Mon–Fri, 18.00–23.30 Sat ⓝ Tram: Porte de Bourgogne

Golden Triangle, Jardin Public, Chartrons & Bacalan

Chic and well-heeled, the Triangle d'Or (Golden Triangle) and the Jardin Public are the places to go for window shopping, admiring both the glamorous objects to buy, and the glamorous Bordelaises enjoying *la belle vie française*. Moving up into Chartrons, things get slightly grungier, as this former merchant and artist quarter has more narrow streets and tiny shops; but it is increasingly trendy and expensive, and now one of the liveliest, most rewarding districts of the city. Bacalan, further up again, is promisingly up and coming but still has a way to go.

SIGHTS & ATTRACTIONS

Allées de Tourny

A pretty square that leads onto the Grand Théâtre. Together they mark the far side of the pedestrianised Old Town, and the crossover into the chic Triangle d'Or district. Some of the city's smartest restaurants are housed around this square, together with the wine school and many wine shops, while the central space has a carousel and hosts the annual summer food fair and winter Christmas fair (see Annual events, page 11). Ⓝ Tram: Grand Théâtre

Basilique Saint-Seurin (Saint-Seurin Basilica)

Just to the north of Gambetta and the city centre is one of the most striking examples of religious architecture you'll find. Recent renovations show off the elaborate carvings inside and out. An 11th-century crypt holds an early-Christian necropolis,

△ *The ornate fountain at place des Quinconces*

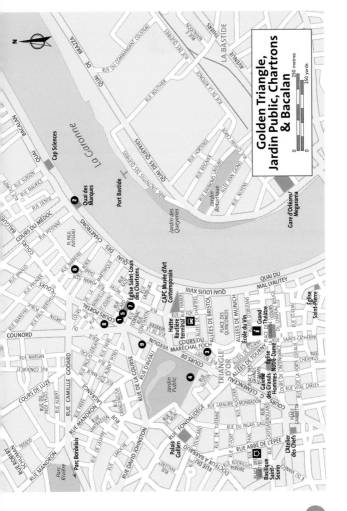

with mausoleums, sarcophagus and frescos. Every Thursday during July and August there is a free concert starting at 18.00. ⓐ pl. des Martyrs de la Résistance ⓛ 08.30–19.00 Tues–Sat, 09.00–12.15, 19.00–20.15 Sun ⓝ Bus: 83

École du Vin

The official wine school of Bordeaux that runs two- and three-hour classes, special courses focusing on food and wine matching or blending, or longer three- or four- dayers that divide their time between the classroom and the vineyards. ⓐ 1 cours du 30 juillet, south of pl. Quinconces off allées de Tourny ⓣ (05) 56 00 22 66 ⓝ Tram: Quinconces

Église Notre-Dame (Notre-Dame Church)

Just next to the Grand Hommes shopping centre, you could easily miss this beautiful, baroque-style church as it's hidden in an attractive square sandwiched between chic clothing shops. Concerts and organ recitals are held regularly. ⓐ pl. du Chapelet, off cours de l'Intendance ⓣ 09 50 64 63 12 ⓛ 08.30–12.00, 14.30–18.00 (closes 18.30 Fri, 19.30 Sat) ⓝ Tram: Grand Théâtre

Église Saint-Louis des Chartrons (Saint Louis de Chartrons Church)

Beautiful Catholic church in the heart of Chartrons, dating back to the 14th century, although the current neo-Gothic structure was constructed in 1880. It holds free concerts most Sunday afternoons. Due to the high number of immigrants traditionally living in Chartrons, from English and Irish merchants to Dutch missionaries, it was known in the 18th century as the 'Foreigners' Church'. ⓐ pl. de Langalerie, off rue Notre-Dame ⓣ (05) 56 00 66 00

CHARTRONS

The area of Chartrons has a colourful history, bound up with immigrants of all nationalities, most often from Ireland, Scotland, England and Holland. They arrived in Bordeaux mainly between the 17th and 18th centuries to trade cocoa, spices, teas, coffees, sugar and wine between Europe, America and the French colonies in Africa and the Caribbean. Buildings such as the CAPC Museum of Contemporary Art began life as an *entrepôt*, or sugar warehouse. At the end of the 19th century, the city's mayor, Lodi-Martin Duffour-Dubergier, proclaimed, '*L'âme de Bordeaux, c'est le commerce*' ('The soul of Bordeaux is trade') – and Chartrons was where most of it went on. As wine merchants moved out of the city centre to expand their warehouses and bottling lines in areas where land was less expensive, so Chartrons spent many years with increasingly blackened walls and empty shop fronts, but today commerce, and plenty of residents, have moved back in, and these few square miles contain some of the highest property prices in the region.

🕐 Office: 14.00–18.00 Mon–Fri 🚊 Tram: Place Paul Doumer; bus: 31, 4

Jardin Public (Public Garden)

Ducks on the pond, classical music on the carousel, a large children's play area, a museum of natural history (closed until

2012), a library, an excellent café, a botanical garden, formal flowerbeds and loads of grass: now that's what we call a park. ⓐ pl. du Champ de Mars; entrances on cours de Verdun, rue du Jardin Public, rue d'Aviau, pl. Bardineau ⓛ 07.00–21.00 summer; 07.00–20.00 spring & autumn; 07.00–18.00 winter ⓝ Tram: Jardin Public; bus: 31

Palais Gallien

Best preserved of the Roman ruins right in the city centre, dating back to the second century. It was originally an amphitheatre capable of holding 17,000 people. It's well hidden down a side street, but worth seeking out, even though only a few walls remain – basically the entrance to the original amphitheatre. ⓐ access on rue du Docteur Albert Barraud ⓛ 14.00–19.00 ⓝ Bus: 53. Admission charge

Parc Bordelais

The largest park in the city, just on the other side of the boulevards by the Barrière du Médoc. There's a river, an animal park, a little train, lots of swans and ducks and a Punch and Judy theatre. ⓐ rue du Bocage. Entrances also on rue du Parc ⓛ 07.00–21.00 summer; 07.00–20.00 spring & autumn; 07.00–18.00 winter ⓝ Bus: 57, 58

Parc Rivière

This is a great place to escape from the city for a few hours. Of particular interest are the ruins of a 19th-century château. ⓐ rue de Rivière ⓛ 07.00–21.00 summer; 07.00–20.00 spring & autumn; 07.00–18.00 winter ⓝ Bus: 27, 57, 58

Place des Quinconces

Among Europe's biggest pedestrianised squares, this elegant, tree-lined expanse features a striking fountain and statues of Montaigne and Montesquieu, two of Bordeaux's most famous sons. ⓐ Esplanade de Quinconces Ⓝ Tram: Quinconces

Quai des Chartrons (Chartrons Quay)

A delightful quay consisting of wide pavements lined with cafés and restaurants running alongside the river. Attractions include a skate park, a children's biking area and some good playgrounds. Ⓝ Tram: Chartrons

CULTURE

Base Sous-Marine (Submarine Pen)

Built by the Nazis during World War II to house their U-boats, this impressive concrete structure is strangely haunting. There's an exhibition of the submarines inside, plus an art gallery as part of the complex, and cultural events and music nights are held regularly. ⓐ blvd Alfred Daney ⓣ (05) 56 11 11 50 Ⓛ 14.00–18.00 Tues–Sat Ⓝ Tram: Bassins à Flot

Cap Sciences

At the far end of the quays, the science and natural history museum is housed in a modern building and contains fun and interactive exhibits on everything from space travel to how computers work. ⓐ Hangar 20, quai Bacalan ⓣ (05) 56 01 07 07 Ⓦ www.cap-sciences.net Ⓛ 14.00–18.00 Tues–Fri, 14.00–19.00 Sat & Sun Ⓝ Tram: Les Hangars

CAPC Musée d'Art Contemporain (Museum of Contemporary Art)

This stunning space has been open since the 1980s, and contains a mix of permanent works (look out for Keith Haring's *Baby in the Lift*) and changing exhibitions. The excellent café does the best Sunday brunch around. ⓐ 7 rue Ferrère ⓣ (05) 56 00 81 50 ⓛ 11.00–18.00 Tues, Thur–Sun, 11.00–20.00 Wed Ⓝ Tram: CAPC. Admission charge

Frac Collection Aquitaine (Frac Gallery)

This is a free exhibition space that regularly holds contemporary photography, sculpture and video exhibits, often favouring regional artists. Since 1983, Frac (regional art collections) have appeared in many cities all over France, created to promote the visual arts as well as decentralising the Paris-based art network. ⓐ Hangar G2, Bassins à Flot no. 1, quai Armand Lalande ⓣ (05) 56 24 71 36 ⓦ www.fracaquitaine.net ⓛ 10.00–18.00 Mon–Fri, 14.00–18.00 Sat Ⓝ Tram: Bassins à Flot

Le Garage Moderne

Proving that the most uplifting things can be found in the most unlikely of places, this unusual building is a working garage that doubles as an exhibition space. You can take your car in to be repaired, get a hands-on lesson in how to repair it, end up discussing your favourite artist or admiring an exhibition of sculptures that is displayed among the rusting bumpers. ⓐ 1 rue des Étrangers ⓣ (05) 56 50 91 33 ⓦ www.legaragemoderne.org ⓛ 09.00–12.00 Mon–Fri, 14.00–19.00 Sat Ⓝ Tram: Bassins à Flot

Grand Théâtre

Perhaps the city's most famous sight, this beautiful building was designed by Victor Hugo and opened in 1780. Corinthean columns line one side, and an art deco-style bar and café serves drinks and

🔺 *Ornate decoration in the atrium of the Grand Théâtre*

bistro-style food. Opera, classical concerts and ballet are performed throughout the year. ⓐ pl. de la Comédie ❶ (05) 56 00 85 90 ⓛ Performance times vary; free public tours 1st Sun of month; call for other tour times ❶ (05) 56 00 66 00 Ⓝ Tram: Grand Théâtre

RETAIL THERAPY

The shopping experience in this area is a pleasantly sedate one. Small antique shops, furniture restorers and larger antique showrooms abound on rue Notre-Dame. Rue Faubourg des Arts, at the top of cours Portal, is a gem: an artists' street, entirely given over to small workshops and artisan boutiques, from sculptures to lighting specialists to seamstresses.

Chez Antoine The best pâtisserie in town, where simple sugar creations turn into little pieces of gourmet heaven. Try their brightly coloured macaroons. ⓐ 19 cours Portal ❶ (05) 56 81 43 19 ⓛ 08.00–20.00 Mon–Sat, 07.30–14.00 Sun Ⓝ Tram: Place Paul Doumer

Comptoir des Cotonniers Find a good range of women's and children's clothing at this stylish boutique. ⓐ 11 rue Jean-Jacques Rousseau ❶ (05) 56 44 76 26 Ⓦ www.comptoirdescotonniers.com ⓛ 10.00–19.00 Mon–Sat Ⓝ Tram: Grand Théâtre

Galerie des Grands Hommes One of the most chic central shopping centres – housed in a glass rotunda, with streets heading off, all named after the *grands hommes* Montesquieu and Voltaire. Inside is a mix of shops hawking food, toys, interiors

and clothes. ⓐ pl. des Grands Hommes ⓛ 10.00–20.00 Mon–Sat
Ⓝ Tram: Grand Théâtre; bus: 4

Jean d'Alos If you want to buy cheese, explore cheese, admire
cheese or sample cheese, this is the place to come. The same shop
has a branch in Chartrons, on cours Portal. ⓐ 4 rue Montesquieu,
off cours de l'Intendance ⓣ (05) 56 44 29 66 ⓛ 15.30–19.15 Mon,
09.00–13.00, 15.00–19.15 Tues–Thur, 09.00–13.00, 14.00–19.15
Fri, 08.30–19.00 Sat Ⓝ Tram: Grand Théâtre; bus: 4

MAC Cosmetics Just one of the many chic shops that line
cours Georges Clémenceau, one of the outer points of the
Triangle d'Or. ⓐ 14 cours Georges Clémenceau ⓣ (05) 57 30 00 00
ⓦ www.maccosmetics.fr ⓛ 10.30–19.00 Tues–Sat Ⓝ Bus: 15

Papeterie de Malherbe North of place Gambetta, this old-
fashioned shop sells a wide range of birthday and Christmas
cards, more stylish and unusual than many you can find in France.
ⓐ 5 rue Huguerie ⓣ (05) 56 48 16 65 ⓦ www.millepapiers.com
ⓛ 08.00–12.40, 13.45–19.00 Tues–Fri, 09.00–12.00, 14.30–19.00
Sat Ⓝ Bus: 15

Pig and Rose Women and children are well catered for in
this fashionable clothes boutique. ⓐ 130 cours de Verdun
ⓣ (05) 56 44 61 39 ⓛ 10.30–13.00, 15.00–19.00 Tues–Sat Ⓝ Bus: 4

TAKING A BREAK

10 Dowling Street £–££ ❶ British-themed coffeeshop, where you

◀ *Relax and watch the world go by in one of the city's many cafés*

can stock up on baked beans and HP Sauce while enjoying their excellent snacks. A good wine selection also, to take away as well as consume on the premises. ⓐ 10 rue Sicard ⓣ (05) 56 01 20 90 ⓦ www.10-dowling-street.info ⓛ 11.30–15.30, 17.30–21.30 Mon–Fri ⓝ Tram: Place Paul Doumer

Comptoir 15 £–££ ❷ A great place for a quick bite to eat by the outlet stores that now line the far end of the quays. There's free WiFi, along with a range of hot and cold tartines. ⓐ Hangar 15, quai des Marques ⓣ (05) 56 01 28 99 ⓦ www.quaidesmarques.com ⓛ 09.30–17.00 Mon–Fri, 09.30–20.00 Sat & Sun ⓝ Tram: Les Hangars

Nulle Part Ailleurs £–££ ❸ Visit this relaxed bar at lunchtime for a good value meal; in the evenings, football fans tend to frequent the place and it becomes considerably rowdier. ⓐ 19 cours du Maréchal Foch ⓣ (05) 56 52 27 58 ⓛ 07.30–22.00 Mon–Fri, 10.00–15.00 Sat ⓝ Tram: Quinconces

L'Orangerie £–££ ❹ Ah! A tea shop in the Jardin Public. Ice-cream coloured chairs outside for relaxing in summer, lots of plants inside to make you feel summery even if it's raining. Cream teas and weekend brunches are available. ⓐ Jardin Public, cours de Verdun ⓣ (05) 56 48 24 41 ⓛ 08.30–19.30 ⓝ Tram: Jardin Public

La Vie en Rose ££ ❺ Fantastic tea shop that serves huge salads, quiches and sweet treats in a restful, feminine atmosphere. ⓐ 8 rue Sicard ⓣ (05) 56 48 03 44 ⓛ 09.00–19.00 Tues–Sat ⓝ Tram: Place Paul Doumer

AFTER DARK

RESTAURANTS

Le Boucher ££ ❻ Meat, meat and more meat, excellently prepared, very faithful crowd. ⓐ 35 rue Borie ❶ (05) 57 87 20 58 ⏱ 19.30–23.00 Tues–Sat ⓝ Tram: Chartrons; bus: 29

Chez Dupont ££ ❼ Classic French bistro with a small number of tables outside. Good range of fish and meat dishes, and almost always a queue. ⓐ 45 rue Notre-Dame ❶ (05) 56 81 49 59 ⏱ 12.00–14.00, 19.30–22.30 Tues–Sat ⓝ Tram: Place Paul Doumer

Influence Wok ££ ❽ Pick and mix your fresh noodles and sauce. ⓐ 23 cours Portal ❶ (05) 57 59 12 17 ⏱ 11.45–14.30 Mon, 11.45–14.30, 19.00–22.00 Tues–Sat ⓝ Tram: Place Paul Doumer

Le 7e Péché £££ ❾ A young German chef is making this new restaurant one of the top eateries in the Chartrons district. Expect gourmet food and imaginative flavour combinations. ⓐ 65 cours Verdun ❶ (05) 56 06 42 16 ⏱ 19.30–22.30 Wed–Mon ⓝ Tram: Place Paul Doumer

La Dame de Shanghai £££ ❿ Glamorous Asian-fusion restaurant housed in an old clipper boat, by the Bassins à Flot. Good bar downstairs that hosts DJ nights from Thursday to Saturday. ⓐ Bassins à Flot no. 1, quai Armand Lalande ❶ (05) 57 10 20 50 ⓦ www.damedeshanghai.com ⏱ 20.00–23.00 Tues–Sun ⓝ Tram: Bassins à Flot

PUBS, BARS & CLUBS

Le Blush Champagne bar and DJ nights give this Bacalan club sophistication. ⓐ Hangar 36, Bassins à Flot no. 1 ⓣ (05) 56 50 40 60 ⓛ 23.00–04.00 Ⓝ Tram: Bassins à Flot

Buzuba A restaurant, bar and beer garden, where something different is always going on, from projecting films onto a big screen, to funk or rare groove DJ nights. ⓐ 1 rue Gironde, Bassins à Flot no. 1 ⓣ (05) 56 50 40 60 or 08 84 62 80 53 ⓛ 12.00–02.00 Wed–Sat Ⓝ Tram: Bassins à Flot

Cambridge Arms British pub that serves hearty fare from pies to fish and chips. ⓐ 27 rue Rode ⓣ (05) 56 51 19 22 ⓛ 11.00–02.00 Ⓝ Tram: Chartrons ; bus: 31

Cave de la Corse The Jardin Public's best-kept secret – a classic neighbourhood off-licence, that sells wine to take away but also to drink on the premises, perched around old wine barrels surrounded by locals. Jazz nights sometimes, chess always. Closing time is flexible depending on how many people are in the bar. ⓐ 43 rue de la Course ⓣ (05) 56 52 62 57 ⓛ 10.30–13.00, 16.30–21.00 Ⓝ Tram: Place Paul Doumer

Molly Malone's Irish pub with great fish and chips and a good spot for watching big matches. ⓐ 83 quai des Chartrons ⓣ (05) 57 87 06 72 ⓦ www.molly-pub.com ⓛ 11.00–02.00 Ⓝ Tram: Chartrons

The Right Bank, Bordeaux Lac, Bouliac & beyond

Until a few years ago, the Right Bank (known as La Bastide), was a no-go area, an industrial wasteland cut off from central Bordeaux by the wide river that flows between the two banks. But big investment – and most importantly the opening of the tram that crosses the Pont de Pierre – has reconnected this interesting area with the other side of the river bank. A new bridge will link Bacalan and Bordeaux by 2014, further connecting this area to the city centre. And the best views of the Bordeaux skyline, especially of place de la Bourse and the Miroir d'Eau at night, come from over here. Behind the Bastide lie some interesting suburbs, especially the pretty village of Bouliac. A little further afield, Bordeaux Lac might not live up to its leafy-sounding name, but there are very attractive open spaces, running tracks and, of course, the lake itself – as well as a large conference centre, a modern casino and a number of shopping centres.

SIGHTS & ATTRACTIONS

Bois de Bordeaux (Bordeaux Woods)

This is the largest single green space in Bordeaux, located right alongside Bordeaux Lac. And this really is green space – parkland, rivers and woods interspersed with more formal arrangements such as children's playgrounds and sports tracks.

ⓐ av. de Pernon, Bordeaux Lac ⓛ 07.00–dusk ⓝ Bus: 31

▶ *The new tramway crosses the old Pont de Pierre*

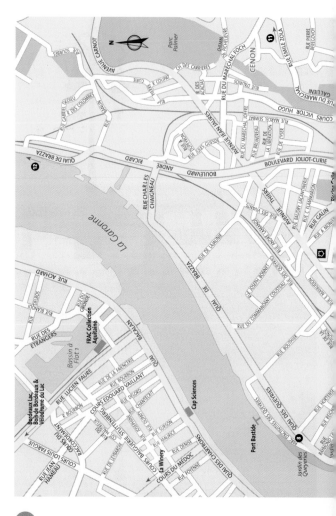

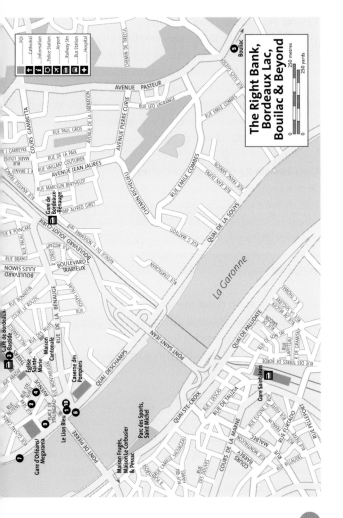

Caserne des Pompiers (Fire Station)

This striking 1950s building – loved and loathed in equal measure – is a firemen's depot that is the subject of several plans for preservation and improvement. Its architecture is modernist and 'ugly' – all corners and bright orange sidings – but compelling, and one of the landmarks that defines the Right Bank. rue de la Benauge Only open on occasional special days; ask at tourist office for details Tram: Stalingrad

Croisières Burdigala (Burgidala Cruises)

Several boat trips are available up and down the river, from Pont de Pierre, including tours of the five bridges of Bordeaux, or simply steaming up and down the quays. Particularly beautiful at sunset. Pont de Pierre (05) 56 49 36 88 or 06 07 19 75 86 www.evolutiongaronne.com Phone to arrange a trip Tram: Stalingrad

Église Sainte-Marie (Saint-Marie Church)

A very attractive church that dates back to the 1860s, with a lofty spire that is lit up beautifully every night. 62 av. Thiers No phone Open for Sunday services & special occasions Tram: Jardin Botanique

Gare d'Orléans/Megarama

Actually no longer a station, but a leisure complex by place de Stalingrad with a cinema, bowling alley, play area and a number of restaurants. 7 quai des Queyries 08 92 69 33 17 www.megarama.fr Varies according to film times, check ahead Tram: Stalingrad

Jardin Botanique (Botanical Garden)

Opened in 2006, this Japanese-influenced botanical garden has several themed 'zones' and has become the focal point of the regeneration of the Right Bank. Among the many points

BORDEAUX'S BRIDGES

There are three main bridges that cross the Garonne in Bordeaux – the Pont de Pierre built in the 1820s, and the Pont d'Aquitaine and the Pont Francois Mitterand, both built after 1960. There is also a steel railway bridge, built in the 1850s by Gustave Eiffel and used daily by hundreds of trains (including the high-speed TGV), and next to it a smaller road bridge. But really the only serious contender to link both banks is the Pont de Pierre – there are 6 km (nearly 4 miles) separating the Pont d'Aquitaine and the Pont de Pierre. This means that the Right Bank is still largely cut off from the Left and cycling or walking between the two means always crossing over at this one point. By car, there are always heavy traffic jams to negotiate (although the tramway that also uses the Pont de Pierre has helped ease traffic enormously). What all this means is that, for now, the regeneration of the Right Bank is very much contained by access to the bridge and its tramline. To improve this situation, a sixth bridge is planned to cross between Bacalan and the Bastide, with an estimated opening date of 2014. It is expected to be called Pont Lucien Faure, and has a projected budget of €120 million. Perhaps they'll get a bridging loan.

of interest is the water garden, with its many plants and large stepping stones. There's also a section where local residents can grow their own vegetables. quai des Queyries (05) 56 52 18 77 08.00–20.00 summer; 08.00–18.00 winter Tram: Jardin Botanique

Jardins des Queyries (Queyries Gardens)

Leading directly off the river bank, this lung of green space provides fantastic views back over place de la Bourse and place des Quinconces. quai des Queyries Tram: Jardin Botanique

Le Lion Bleu, place de Stalingrad

One of the most striking sculptures in the city, this huge statue of a blue lion was created by sculptor Xavier Veilhan, and has proved very popular with local children, who often try to jump off his giant paws. pl. de Stalingrad Tram: Stalingrad

Maison Cantonale

A striking art nouveau building dating from 1926 (it was intended to be built a decade earlier, but World War I got in the way). Today it houses a library, the local mayor's office and a police station. Concerts are occasionally staged here. 42 rue des Nuits (05) 56 86 20 56 Mayor's office: 09.00–12.30, 13.00–16.30 Tram: Jardin Botanique

Maison Le Corbusier

This run-down but interesting road is one of Le Corbusier's social housing projects, constructed in 1927, where he took the same principles of industrial design, simple geometric spaces

◯ *Take a boat trip for a riverside perspective of the city*

and clean aesthetics and applied them to low-cost housing.
They haven't been kept particularly smart, but one is open
as a museum. Die-hard architecture fans will appreciate this
place the most. ⓐ 4 rue Le Corbusier, Pessac ⓣ (05) 56 36 56 46
ⓛ 14.00–18.00 Wed–Fri, 14.00–18.30 Sat & Sun

Piscine Galin (Galin swimming pool)
Public swimming pool that has a retractable roof for summer
time. ⓐ 3 rue Galin ⓣ (05) 56 86 25 01 ⓛ 12.00–14.00, 17.00–19.00
Mon, Tues & Thur, 10.00–12.00, 15.00–20.00 Wed, 09.00–13.00
Sat & Sun ⓝ Tram: Thiers Benauge

🔺 *Practice sessions at the Vélodrome*

Pont de Pierre

The oldest bridge that crosses the Garonne from place de Stalingrad to place Bir Hakeim, built in 1822. Its elegant arches and entire 490 m (1,608 ft) are lit by traditional lamps and larger floodlights when night falls. ⓦ Tram: Stalingrad or Port de Bourgogne

Vélodrome du Lac

Cycling competitions are held at this excellent track on a regular basis, but there is plenty of opportunity to use it for leisure cycling as well as skating, tennis and bowling. ⓐ cours Jules Ladoumègue ⓣ (05) 56 43 16 05 ⓦ www.axelvega.com ⓛ Varies according to event ⓦ Bus: 31

La Winery

Located about a 20-minute drive from central Bordeaux is this modern winery with a restaurant, tasting bar, regular concerts and a large shop selling wines from around the world. If you want to 'do' wine, this is the place to come. ⓐ Rond-point des Vendangeurs, Départementale 1, Arsac-en-Médoc ⓣ (05) 56 39 04 90 ⓦ www.la-winery.fr ⓛ 10.00–19.00 ⓦ Train: Gare Saint-Jean to Margaux, then ten minutes by taxi

RETAIL THERAPY

Boutique Bernard Magrez Château Pape Clément's wine shop, located just outside the château in the outlying suburb of Pessac. Call in advance to organise a tour and tasting session; this place is seriously glamorous. ⓐ Château Pape Clément, 216 av. du Docteur

Nancel Penard, Pessac ☎ (05) 57 26 43 04 🕐 11.00–18.00 Mon–Sat
🚌 Bus: 46, 47, 48

TAKING A BREAK

Délices et Café – Bordeaux Bastide £ ❶ Good spot for
breakfast or a snack lunch, with a wide range of herbal teas
and always at least two different *plats du jour* (dishes of
the day) on offer. 📍 pl. de Stalingrad ☎ (05) 56 52 19 71
🕐 09.00–19.30 Mon–Fri, 10.00–19.30 Sat 🚊 Tram: Stalingrad

Les Temps Modernes £–££ ❷ Close to the Megarama cinema,
this cheerful café/bistro offers non-stop service, with larger
lunches and dinners served at midday and in the evenings.
📍 27 rue Sainte-Marie ☎ (05) 56 40 50 78 🕐 10.00–15.00,
19.30–22.00 Mon–Sat 🚊 Tram: Stalingrad

O Sombre Héros ££ ❸ Traditional French food is on offer at
this friendly bar, along with 30 different types of Spanish tapas.
Both French and Spanish wines are available. 📍 96 av. Thiers
☎ (05) 56 32 82 58 🕐 12.00–02.00 🚊 Tram: Jardin Botanique

AFTER DARK

RESTAURANTS
La Mama £–££ ❹ Great pizza restaurant in a striking building.
The pizzas have thin, crispy bases, tasty toppings and arrive fresh
from a wood-fired oven. 📍 1 rue Sainte-Marie ☎ (05) 57 54 02 19
🕐 12.00–14.30, 19.00–23.00 Mon–Sat 🚊 Tram: Stalingrad

Café de L'Espérance ££ ❺ Set in the pretty village of Bouliac, right by the Saint James Hotel, this is an upmarket bistro. The relaxed atmosphere is enhanced with great meat dishes and a groaningly good dessert trolley. ❹ 33 rue de l'Esplanade ❶ (05) 56 20 52 16 ❷ 12.00–14.00, 20.00–22.00 ❸ Bus: 7

Café du Port ££ ❻ Large dining room overlooking the Garonne, with wooden tables, green plants and 1930s posters around the walls. Good range of seafood and gourmet meat dishes. ❹ 1 quai Deschamps ❶ (05) 56 77 81 18 ❷ 12.00–14.00, 19.00–22.00 ❸ Tram: Stalingrad

L'Estacade ££ ❼ Restaurant on wooden stilts with one of the best views in town – directly back over the river to the Miroir d'Eau and place de la Bourse. Seafood is particularly good here, but the food takes second place to the setting. Excellent wine list. ❹ quai des Queyries ❶ (05) 57 54 02 50 ❷ 12.00–14.00, 19.30–22.30 Mon–Sat, 12.00–14.00, 19.30–21.30 Sun ❿ www.lestacade.com ❸ Tram: Stalingrad

La Petite Gironde ££ ❽ Regular jazz and live music nights make this restaurant particularly appealing. ❹ 75 quai des Queyries ❶ (05) 57 80 33 33 ❷ 12.00–14.30, 20.00–22.30 Mon–Fri, 20.00–22.30 Sat, 12.00–14.30 Sun ❸ Tram: Stalingrad

Royal Bastide ££ ❾ One of the few Chinese restaurants on the Right Bank. ❹ 7 quai des Queyries ❶ (05) 56 86 88 99 ❷ 12.00–14.30, 19.00–23.30 ❸ Tram: Stalingrad

Le Wasabi Café ££ ⑩ Japanese restaurant with an excellent range of super-fresh sushi. ⓐ 3 pl. de Stalingrad ⓣ (05) 56 32 28 44 ⓛ 12.00–14.00, 19.00–22.30 Mon–Fri, 12.00–14.00, 19.00–23.00 Sat ⓝ Tram: Stalingrad

La Cape £££ ⑪ Located in the residential suburb of Cenon, this is a Michelin-starred restaurant and a real find. The colourful decoration and artistically displayed food make this a sensory overload at times, but the meals are certainly memorable. ⓐ 9 allée de la Morlette, Cenon ⓣ (05) 57 80 24 25 ⓛ 12.00–13.30, 20.00–21.30 Mon–Fri, 20.00–21.30 Sat ⓝ Tram: Cenon Gare

Le Château du Prince Noir (Restaurant Jean Marie Amat) £££ ⑫ A Michelin-starred restaurant run by renowned chef Jean Marie Amat. Expect a beautifully crafted and very fresh, seasonal menu from one of the region's most interesting characters. ⓐ 26 rue Raymond Lis, Lormont ⓣ (05) 56 06 12 52 ⓛ 12.00–14.00, 20.00–21.30 Mon–Fri, 20.00–21.30 Sat ⓝ Tram: Lormont Lauriers; bus: 66

PUBS, BARS & CLUBS
Central Pub English-style pub with good range of beers and snacks – and the great advantage of continual service, unlike many places in Bordeaux. Gets lively later. ⓐ 7 quai des Queyries ⓣ (05) 57 80 38 00 ⓛ 12.00–02.00 ⓝ Tram: Stalingrad

Chez Alriq Coffees and teas are equally as good as the beers and wines at this relaxed *guingette* (riverside café). There are concerts every night during the summer. ⓐ Port Bastide,

○ *L'Estacade has a prime location on the banks of the Garonne River*

quai des Queyries ❶ (05) 56 86 58 49 ❷ 19.00–02.00 Thur–Sat, Apr–Oct; also open some winter weekends ❷ Tram: Stalingrad

L'Eclypse Large club with a slightly older clientele, often with themed evenings. Can hold up to 1,000 clubbers, so any visiting DJs get a good reception. Located on the outskirts of the Bastide, on the road out to Bouliac. ❸ 6 rue Jean Dupas, quai de la Souys ❶ (05) 56 86 64 31 ❿ www.eclypse-bordeaux.com ❷ 22.00–04.00 Fri & Sat ❷ Tram: Stalingrad, then 10-min walk. Admission charge

Krakatoa Small, crowded and atmospheric concert venue where the likes of Kaiser Chiefs and Air have played. Concerts finish at midnight. ❸ 3 av. Victor Hugo, Mérignac Arlac ❶ (05) 56 24 34 29 ❿ www.krakatoa.org ❷ Times vary according to event; check listings or call ahead ❷ Tram: Mérignac Centre; bus: 50. Admission charge

Modern'Bar Smart bar with plenty of mirrors and polished brass. Good choice of beers. ❸ 18 av. Thiers ❶ (05) 56 86 35 55 ❷ 06.30–20.00 ❷ Tram: Stalingrad

● *The vineyards of Saint Émillion*

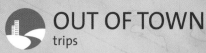
OUT OF TOWN
trips

Coastal resorts: Arcachon, Pyla & Cap Ferret

Just under an hour (or significantly more if caught in summer traffic) away from Bordeaux is the Atlantic Coast and the popular resorts of Arcachon, Pyla and Cap Ferret. Moving further up the coast there are a number of very good beaches, and even some large inland lakes that offer great water sports opportunities. Moving south of Arcachon, towards (eventually) Biarritz and the Spanish border, there are some fun surf resorts such as Mimizan. Wherever you choose to explore, the whole coast is a mixture of pine trees, beaches and sand dunes, and there are well-developed cycle and jogging paths that line the entire coastline.

GETTING THERE

From the Gare Saint-Jean (see page 46), there are at least three return train services every day to Arcachon, and more in July and August.

To drive to Arcachon, take the A63 motorway from Bordeaux, then the A660 to Arcachon. For Le Porge take exit 23 off the A63 motorway by Marcheprime, then follow signs to Le Temple and Le Porge. For Pyla, take A63 motorway from Bordeaux. Then take the A660 towards Arcachon, the N250 and finally the D259 signposted Pyla.

Regular buses run from Arcachon to Pyla; times vary according to day and season so ask at the bus station. A free yellow bus known as 'ého!' circulates through Arcachon city centre.

🔻 *Aerial view of Cap Ferret bay*

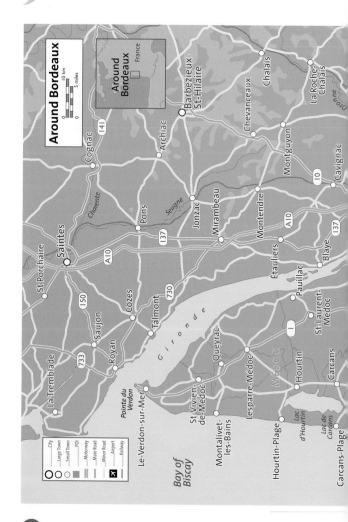

Around Bordeaux

Around Bordeaux

France

| 0 | 10 km |
| 0 | 5 miles |

Barbezieux-St-Hilaire

Chalais

La Roche-Chalais

Chevanceaux

Dronne

Cognac

141

Archiac

Montguyon

Cavignac

10

Chente

Pons

Seugne

Jonzac

Mirambeau

Montendre

137

Saintes

A10

137

Etauliers

A10

Blaye

St Porchaire

Cozes

730

Talmont

Pauillac

St-Laurent-Médoc

150

Saujon

G i r o n d e

Queyrac

MÉDOC

1

La Tremblade

733

Royan

St-Vivien-de-Médoc

Lesparre-Médoc

Hourtin

Carcans

Pointe du Verdon

Le-Verdon-sur-Mer

Montalivet-les-Bains

Hourtin-Plage

Lac d'Hourtin

Lac de Carcans

Carcans-Plage

Bay of Biscay

City
Large Town
Small Town
POI
Motorway
Main Road
Minor Road
Airport
Railway

106

SIGHTS & ATTRACTIONS

La Chapelle de la Villa Algérienne

A beautiful chapel located at the far end of the beach in the pretty oyster village of l'Herbe. It was once attached to the grand Villa Algérienne (now largely destroyed, although small parts of the façade remain). It is not open to the public except on special days; contact the tourist office for details. ⓐ route du Cap Ferret, l'Herbe

Dune de Pyla

Europe's highest sand dune stands at 105 metres (344 feet) tall. It overlooks the Arcachon Bassin (a sheltered inland bay), about 5 km (3 miles) from Arcachon town. From the top, you get great views over the bay to Cap Ferret on the far side. The dune in total is 2,500 metres (8,202 feet) long and 500 metres (1,640 feet) wide, and its slope is between 30° and 40° on the east side, and between 5° and 20° on the west. But don't worry; someone has kindly put a staircase in the side of the dune for climbing up to the top, from where you can walk for miles, admiring the view of boats in the bay. To get back down again, nothing beats running as fast as you can... ⓦ www.dune-pyla.com

Ets Charbonnier

Boat hire, but also scuba diving and fishing trips are available here. The same agency also rents out bikes for exploring the many bike paths that line the Cap. ⓐ 51 av. de l'Océan, Cap Ferret ⓣ (05) 56 60 61 87 ⓦ www.etscharbonnier.fr

● *The vast expanse of sand at Dune de Pyla*

L'Île aux Oiseaux

'Bird Island', off the coast of Cap Ferret, takes its name from its large population of herons, geese and moorhens. There are also around 40 oyster farmer huts on the island, two of which are suspended on poles (*cabanes tchanquées*, from the Gascon word for stilt). Although you can't actually go on shore, you can take a boat trip around it with **Bateliers Arcachonnais** (ⓐ 76 blvd de la Plage, Arcachon ⓣ (557) 722 828 ⓦ www.bateliers-arcachon.com). They run boat trips several times a day during the summer, leaving from the Cap Ferret pier, but times vary according to season and tides so call in advance.

Lège Cap Ferret

Cap Ferret (or 'Les 44 Hectares' as the locals call it, referring to the size of the peninsula) is *the* upmarket holiday spot of choice for smart Bordelais. The whole place is a narrow strip of sand and land that extends 19 km (12 miles) from top to bottom, and in summer châteaux owners and wine merchants decamp here en masse. Among the attractions are a beautiful lighthouse, a beach on 'The Point' (La Pointe) that is located where the sheltered bay turns into the Atlantic Ocean, causing waves that get a lot bigger and more dramatic. There are also lots of great restaurants, and a number

OYSTERS

Oyster parks cover huge areas around the Bassin, and there are over 350 individual businesses and farmers. All over the coastline, you'll find roadside stalls selling freshly shucked oysters. Most are sold direct from producers who have been up since dawn hauling them out of their beds. Arcachon oysters generally cost less than €5 for a dozen, and are more delicate than the colder-water oysters from Normandy, less salty than many from the Mediterranean. As they are farmed oysters, they are available year round – the old adage that you can only eat oysters in a month with an 'R' in it doesn't hold true here. But whatever the month, the best way of serving them is with a squeeze of lemon, a few lightly vinegared shallots, and of course a glass of white wine. Another typical serving suggestion of the southwest is with a spicy chitterling sausage on the side.

of chic clothes and food shops. It's possible to get to Cap Ferret by road or by boat from Arcachon. Just be warned that in summer time, the single road that leads to the Cap can get very over-crowded – you're best to leave either very early in the morning, or very late at night. ⓐ Tourist office: 1 av. du Général de Gaulle, Lège Cap Ferret ⓣ (05) 56 03 94 49 ⓦ www.lege-capferret.com

The Médoc Lakes

There are three main lakes further up the coast from Cap Ferret and Le Porge towards the mouth of the estuary: Lac de Lacanau, Lac de Carcans and Lac d'Hourtin. All three are large and shallow, making for a safe environment for learning windsurfing or sailing. Inevitably this makes them very popular with families. All of the lakes, particularly Lacanau, are really unspoilt. Lac de Lacanau is lined with pine trees and has some lovely beaches. There are places to hire boats to sail around and investigate the coves and hidden bays. If you go right up to the Pointe du Verdon, you're at the far end of the Médoc where there are sailing clubs, mountain bike circuits and plenty of walking routes.

Oyster farmers

All over the Bassin you'll find oyster farmers, oyster huts, oyster festivals – these are particularly prevalent in Gujan-Mestras, Jacquets, Piraillan and l'Herbe. It's always worth driving into these villages, because you'll regularly run into an *ostréiculteur* who is happy to talk about the oysters, show you how to open them correctly, match them with wine – and even, if you're very lucky, to organise a special trip out on a boat to the farms.

Le Phare de Cap Ferret (Cap Ferret Lighthouse)

From the top of this 53 m (174 ft) lighthouse, the view really is spectacular. Photography exhibitions are often held on the lower floors. ● No phone ● 10.00–19.30 July & Aug; 10.00–12.30, 14.00–18.00 May, June & Sept; 14.00–17.00 Wed–Sun, Oct–Mar. Admission charge

Le Porge

A beach on the Atlantic coast, higher up than Cap Ferret but only 45 minutes from Bordeaux, with a long stretch of sand, lots of water sports and good spots for picnicking. It's wilder and more romantic than the perfectly manicured Arcachon beaches, and makes a great spot for walking and sand-castle building. ● Tourist office, 3 pl. St Seurin, Le Porge ● (05) 56 26 54 34 ● www.leporge.fr

RETAIL THERAPY

Antic Art & Déco Great place for browsing for gift ideas, or beautiful things for your house – a mix of antique and modern furniture, plus lamps and even sweets. ● 75 route de Bordeaux, Petit-Piquey, Lège Cap Ferret ● (05) 56 60 91 02 ● www.anticartdeco.com ● 10.00–19.00 Mon–Sat

TAKING A BREAK

La Cabane d'Edouard £ You just can't leave Cap Ferret without stopping at an oyster-tasting hut, and this is one of the best. ● Port de Claouey, Cabanes 1 & 3, Lège Cap Ferret ● (05) 57 70 30 44 ● 12.30–01.30 June–Sept; times vary so call to check

⬥ *Fishing boat moored beside an oyster farm in Arcachon Bay*

Café de la Plage £–££ The same building houses restaurant
Chez Pierre, and both make the most of their excellent location
with a large terrace. The atmosphere is relaxed and chic.
As you'd expect, good seafood – but excellent breakfasts also.
🅰 1 blvd Veyrier Montagnères, Arcachon 🕿 (05) 56 22 52 94
🖮 http://cafedelaplage.com 🕒 12.00–14.30, 19.00–23.00

Eden Gourmands £–££ If you discover this place too early during
your stay in Cap Ferret, you might be going back carrying a few extra
pounds, thanks to the handmade pâtisseries, chocolates and ice
creams. 🅰 64 route de Bordeaux, Lège Cap Ferret 🕿 (05 56 60 51 38
🖮 www.edengourmands-chez-patachou.com 🕒 07.00–13.00,
15.30–20.00 summer; 07.30–13.00, 15.30–19.00 winter

AFTER DARK

Le Panorama £–££ This restaurant might be on a campsite, but
it has one of the best views in Bordeaux. Overlooking the Banc
d'Arguin nature reserve by the Dune de Pyla, you get to watch
the sun go down over white sand, blue seas and circling
sea birds. 🅰 route de Biscarosse, Pyla 🕿 (05) 56 54 40 06
🖮 www.camping-panorama.com 🕒 12.00–14.00, 19.00–23.00

Chez Hortense ££–£££ The best known fish restaurant on the
Bassin overlooks the water and has a very relaxed atmosphere.
The food is wonderful, especially the speciality, *moules* (mussels).
And don't just wait till after dark for this – the view over the Bassin
makes lunchtimes particularly special. 🅰 av. du Semaphore, Lège
Cap Ferret 🕿 (05) 56 60 62 56 🕒 12.00–14.00, 19.00–23.00 Wed–Mon

Le Sail Fish ££–£££ A lovely restaurant with a fresh, airy feel and plenty of lounging areas. ⓐ 38 rue Bernaches, Lège Cap Ferret ⓣ (05) 56 60 44 84 ⓦ www.chezgreg.fr ⓛ 19.30–23.00 July & Aug; 19.30–23.00 Fri & Sat, May, June & Sept

ACCOMMODATION

Hôtel de la Plage, Cap Ferret £–££ Simple and well located on the Atlantic beach side of Cap Ferret. ⓐ 1 av. des Marins, L'Herbe ⓣ (05) 56 60 50 15 ⓛ Mid-Feb–Dec

La Pergola, Arcachon £–££ A guesthouse that offers excellent value in the middle of Arcachon. Not exactly imaginatively decorated rooms, but clean, many with terraces and views. ⓐ 40 cours Lamarque-de-Plaisance ⓣ (05) 56 83 07 89 ⓦ www.hotel-lapergola.net

Hôtel des Dunes ££ A 14-room hotel boasting a sauna, Wi-Fi and a great location near the village and beaches of Cap Ferret. ⓐ 119 av. de Bordeaux, Cap Ferret ⓣ (05) 56 60 61 81 ⓦ www.hoteldesdunes.com ⓛ Feb–Dec

Maison du Bassin, Cap Ferret ££–£££ This place is only open six months of the year, and books up far in advance, but it's wonderful. The décor is New England in feel, laid back but with real attention to detail. There's also a great restaurant and bar serving homemade rums. ⓐ 5 rue des Pionniers ⓣ (05) 56 60 60 63 ⓦ www.lamaisondubassin.com

The vineyards of the Saint Émilion region

If you don't want the beach, head out instead to the vineyards and the beautiful medieval town of Saint Émilion. This lies to the east of the city, about half an hour from Bordeaux towards the Dordogne Valley, and contains some of its most attractive landscapes, with gently undulating hills and miles of vineyards interspersed with small villages, woods and plenty of churches and historical monuments. It can be hard to get into some of the more prestigious wine properties such as Château Petrus or Château Cheval Blanc, but there are lots of winemakers who are only too happy to show you around and share a tasting – and make sure you include at least one whose barrels are stored in an underground cellar, dug out of the limestone hillsides (most of the buildings along the riverfront in Bordeaux centre, incidentally, were made from limestone taken out of quarries around Saint Émilion).

GETTING THERE

There are several trains per day running between Gare Saint-Jean in Bordeaux and Gare Saint-Émilion along the Bordeaux-Sarlat line. Journey time is around 40 minutes; for timetables see ⓦ www.ter-sncf.com or ask at the station.

If you are driving, take the N89 road from Bordeaux to Libourne and continue along until the Libourne Est–Saint Émilion exit on the D243 road.

❍ *The striking church spire in Saint Émilion*

SIGHTS & ATTRACTIONS

Abbaye de La Sauve-Majeure (Sauve-Majeure Abbey)

Eleventh-century Benedictine monastery, now in ruins but with the tower well preserved. You can walk to the top for fantastic views. ⓐ 2 rue de L'Abbaye, La Sauve-Majeure ⓣ (05) 56 23 01 55 ⓛ 10.00–18.00 Apr–Sept; 10.30–13.00, 14.00–17.30 Tues–Sun, Oct–May. Admission charge

La Bataille de Castillon (Battle of Castillon re-enactment)

On 17 July 1453, English forces were finally driven from Aquitaine after losing this historic battle in the Hundred Years' War. Every July and August, the thrashing of the English is re-enacted over a number of weekends. It's great fun to watch, with horses pounding over distant hills, a two-hour show performed on a massive stage and fireworks to end the night. ⓐ 5 allées de la République, Castillon-la-Bataille ⓣ (05) 57 40 1 4 53 ⓦ www.batailledecastillon.com

Castillon-la-Bataille

A smart but quiet town full of lovely 18th-century architecture and a few upmarket shops (it's particularly good for foodies, as there are a number of well-stocked grocery shops and delis). Nice views also, as the town is right on the banks of the Dordogne River.

Cycling & walking paths

There are great cycling paths all over Bordeaux, and this one – going from Sauveterre-de-Guyenne, through Créon and back into Bordeaux – is one of the prettiest, allowing you to ride alongside

UNESCO WORLD HERITAGE
Both Saint Émilion and Bordeaux are now UNESCO World Heritage Sites. This means that the World Heritage Committee considers them to possess a cultural pedigree of universal value. Their reason for classifying Saint Émilion is that it's 'an outstanding example of an historic vineyard landscape that has survived intact and in activity to the present day'. For Bordeaux, the committee commended the fact that, 'its urban form represents the success of philosophers who wanted to make towns into melting pots of humanism, universality and culture'.

vineyards for most of the way. ⓐ Railway station, blvd Victor-Hugo, Créon ⓘ (05) 57 34 30 95 ⓦ http://creonstationvelos.free.fr

Entre Deux Mers
Entre Deux Mers, which literally means 'Between Two Seas', covers the large area to the south of the city, from the right bank of the Garonne over Saint Émilion and the Dordogne. Some of the prettiest villages to look out for include Sauveterre-de-Guyenne, Branne and Monségur.

Libourne
This is a Bastide town with pretty quays and a central square, place Abel Surchamps, that was once fortified and still has elegant arcades. There are also some beautiful quays, where, in the 18th century, wine from Saint Émilion, Pomerol and Entre

deux Mers was loaded onto flat-bottomed barges and sent off to northern France and further afield in Europe.

Planète Bordeaux

A great place to come to learn about the history of winemaking. It's recently been updated and made far more interactive and fun, with a children's play area. Over 1,000 wines are available to buy. ⓐ RN 89, exit 5, Beychac et Cailleau ⓣ (05) 57 97 19 36 ⓦ www.maisondesbordeaux.com ⓛ 10.00–19.00 (last admission 18.00) May–Oct; 09.30–12.00, 14.00–17.30 Nov–Apr. Admission charge

Pujols-sur-Dordogne

Village with status 'prettiest village in France'. Lots of flowers lining the streets, an attractive church and a square with good views over the Dordogne Valley.

Saint Émilion

The most tourist-friendly town in the Bordeaux region, this eighth-century medieval village has been a UNESCO World Heritage Site since 1999. It takes its name from a Breton monk who settled in a grotto in the forest that at the time covered the town's hill. A village grew up around him, as he fasted, prayed and generally performed miracles. You can still visit the original Émilion cave today, plus the many underground monuments that have grown up around his legend, most impressively the monolithic church and catacombs. Above ground, the buildings are carved out of the butter-coloured limestone that was the result of all these religious (and, later, practical) excavations. The town itself is based around two main squares – place du Clocher and place du Marché, and it's a great place for eating and shopping, and, of course, wine tasting.

Tonnellerie du Monde
A fascinating opportunity to see wine barrels being made. You'll get a whole new appreciation of the importance that wood plays in ageing wine. ⓐ 8 route de Canteloup, Beychac et Cailleau ⓣ (05) 56 72 82 00 ⓦ www.tonnelleriedumonde.fr ⓛ By appointment only Mon–Fri

CULTURE

Musée Souterrain de la Poterie (Underground Pottery Museum)
There are over 6,000 exhibits here, with pottery ranging from over 20 centuries of local history. ⓐ Hospices de la Madeleine, 21 rue André Loiseau, Saint Émilion ⓣ (05) 57 24 60 93 ⓦ www.saint-emilion-museepoterie.fr ⓛ 10.00–19.00. Admission charge

RETAIL THERAPY

Comptoir des Vignobles Well-stocked wine shop in the heart of the village, with lots of old vintages and English-speaking staff. Not cheap, but a good place to browse for famous names. ⓐ 1 rue des Girondins, Saint Émilion ⓣ (05) 57 24 61 10 ⓦ www.comptoirvignobles.com ⓛ 10.00–19.00

Libourne Covered Market The covered market in Libourne is worth a visit for its fresh produce and excellent cheese stand, La Ronde

des Fromages. ⓐ 1 rue de Montesquieu, Libourne 🕐 06.00–12.30 Mon–Sat, 06.00–13.30 Sun

Les Macarons de Saint Émilion The Harrods of macaroon emporia. ⓐ rue Guadet, Saint Émilion ☎ (05) 57 24 72 33 🕐 09.30–12.00, 14.30–18.00

TAKING A BREAK

Le Just-en Face £–££ A friendly tapas bar and brasserie offering some good wines by the glass. ⓐ 2 ter, rue Porte Brunet, Saint Émilion ☎ (05) 57 24 79 82 🕐 09.00–02.00 Thur–Mon

Café Guingette ££ Outside tables along the river front in Libourne, with a good selection of salads and fish. Open summer only,

🔻 *Laid-back café culture in Saint Émilion*

and lunchtime only. 13 quai du Général d'Amade, Libourne
🕿 (05) 57 51 87 87 🕘 12.00–14.00 May–Aug

L'Essentiel ££ Slick wine-tasting bar in Saint Émilion, where you can
try big-name châteaux vintages by the glass. 🅐 6 rue Guadet, Saint
Émilion 🕿 (05) 57 24 39 76 🆆 www.essentiel-vin.com 🕘 11.00–20.00

L'Envers du Décor ££ Very popular restaurant with an excellent
wine list and a sheltered courtyard for sunny days. 🅐 11 rue du
Clocher, Saint Émilion 🕿 (05) 57 74 48 31 🕘 12.00–14.30, 19.00–22.30

AFTER DARK

L'Atmosphère, St Germain du Puch ££ Jazz music, great menu,
summery feel with greenery all over… really worth driving for
(15 mins via the A631, N230, E70). 🅐 99 Le Bourg, St Germain
du Puch 🕿 (05) 57 24 52 34 🕘 10.30–15.00, 19.00–01.00

La Poudette ££ Seasonal produce and market finds dominate
the menu at this lovely restaurant. 🅐 1 Bernadigot, Pujols-sur-
Dordogne 🕿 (05) 57 40 71 52 🆆 www.la-poudette.com
🕘 12.00–13.30, 19.30–21.30 Wed–Sun

ACCOMMODATION

Château Hôtel Isabeau de Naujan ££ Recently-restored wine
château that has some lovely rooms and a good restaurant.
🅐 Domaine de Naujan, Saint Vincent de Pertignas
🕿 (05) 57 55 14 30 🆆 www.domaine-de-naujan.com

⬬ *The Château de Sanse is one of the area's prettiest hotels*

Château du Petit Puch ££ Charming place to stay where you can experience a genuine winemaking château. The four rooms are located in one wing of the property. ⓐ St Germain du Puch ⓣ (05) 57 24 52 36 ⓦ www.chateaupetitpuch.com

Château de Sanse ££ Near to Castillon and St Foy La Grande, this 18th-century château has been stylishly refurbished and has good views from the restaurant over the surrounding countryside. ⓐ Ste Radegonde ⓣ (05) 57 56 41 10 ⓦ www.chateaudesanse.com

---

▶ *The tramway is a relaxing and efficient way to get around the city*

PRACTICAL
information

Directory

GETTING THERE

By air

Bordeaux-Mérignac Airport (see page 46) is served by many airlines, including:

Aer Lingus ☏ (01) 70 20 00 72 ⓦ www.aerlingus.com

Air France ☏ 08 20 82 08 20 ⓦ www.airfrance.fr

BMI ☏ (01) 41 91 87 04 ⓦ www.flybmi.com

British Airways ☏ 08 25 82 54 00 ⓦ www.britishairways.com

easyJet ☏ 08 25 08 25 08 ⓦ www.easyjet.com

The flight time from London is approximately 75 minutes.

Many people are aware that air travel emits CO_2, which contributes to climate change. You may be interested in the possibility of lessening the environmental impact of your flight through **Climate Care** (ⓦ www.climatecare.org), which offsets your CO_2 by funding environmental projects around the world.

By rail

The rail journey from London St Pancras International via Eurostar to Paris Gare du Nord, and then by TGV from Paris to Bordeaux should take about six hours in total (trains run regularly throughout the day).

Eurostar for cross-Channel trains ☏ 08705 186 186 ⓦ www.eurostar.com

SNCF for trains within France ☏ 08 92 35 35 35 ⓦ www.voyages-sncf.com

Thomas Cook European Rail Timetable ☏ (01733) 416 477 ⓦ www.thomascookpublishing.com

By road

From Calais, the A1 goes down to Bordeaux, and the car journey should total around eight hours. For driving from the UK via Calais – and thus via **Eurotunnel** (☎ 08705 353 535 ⓦ www.eurotunnel.com) you should make it down in one day, with stops. From northern Spain, you should reach Bordeaux in three hours.

Remember to bring both parts of your driving licence and to inform your insurance company before driving to France. You should carry a copy of your insurance certificate as well as a reflective safety jacket and warning triangles. You will be fined if police stop you without these.

🔺 *Pont de Pierre by night*

When you've arrived in the region, information on traffic is available on ☎ (05) 61 12 77 77.

If you fancy making the trip by coach, **Eurolines** (🌐 www.eurolines.com), Europe's largest coach operator, serves all of France and the rest of the Continent.

By water

The nearest international ferry port is in Caen. Bordeaux is then a six-hour drive from Caen. Alternatively, you can take a ferry to Santander in Spain and drive up (about five hours drive time).

Brittany Ferries ☎ 08 25 82 88 28 🌐 www.brittany-ferries.com

P&O Ferries ☎ 08705 980 333 🌐 www.poferries.com

ENTRY FORMALITIES

EU citizens can travel to France without a visa but require a passport or (for non-UK citizens) an identity card. For USA, Canada, Australia, New Zealand, South Africa, visits of up to three months do not require a visa.

Residents of UK, Ireland and other EU countries may bring into France personal possessions and goods for personal use, provided they have been bought in the EU (and therefore no luggage that contains goods intended for sale as these would be subject to import taxes). For full regulations and definitions of 'reasonable amounts' visit 🌐 www.douane.gouv.fr.

For taking animals to France, the same rules apply as with the rest of the EU (ie they need a European (EU) Pet Passport). All vets should have the relevant information and be able to get your animal ready for travelling with you.

MONEY

The currency of France is the euro (€). 1 euro = 100 cents (also called eurocents). Euros come in notes of €5, €10, €20, €50, €100, €200, €500. Coins are in denominations of €1 and €2, and in cents worth 1c, 2c, 5c, 10c, 20c and 50c. For current exchange rates, check ⓦ www.travelex.com or ⓦ www.oanda.com.

ATM machines are plentiful in Bordeaux and are the easiest way to withdraw money while you're there. Traveller's cheques and foreign money can be cashed at most banks, bureaux de change and some hotels. You will need your passport as identification. Major international credit cards are accepted in most large stores and restaurants and in ATM machines.

HEALTH, SAFETY & CRIME

Drinking water is safe, and many public parks have drinking fountains (if not it is marked *Eau Non Potable*, or 'Water Not for Drinking'). There are plenty of hospitals and doctors, and medical facilities in Bordeaux are excellent.

No inoculations are necessary for travelling to France. If you have any queries, it's always worth asking your doctor before leaving, or reading the Department of Health advice in your home country. In the UK, info is on ⓦ www.dh.gov.uk (in the Travel Advice section). It's always advisable to take a small first-aid kit with you, and keep it in the car if you are travelling around.

Pharmacies are easily found – look for the green crosses – and available throughout the city. One of the most convenient is **Pharmacie de la Bourse** (ⓐ 3 quai Richelieu ⓣ (05) 56 90 94 04 ⓛ 09.00–13.00, 14.00–19.30 Mon–Fri, 10.00–13.00, 15.00–19.30 Sat).

A European Health Insurance Card (EHIC) entitles you to reduced-cost medical treatment in France. Take the card with you for treatment; you will be required to pay on the spot but can reclaim a percentage of the cost when you are back in your home country. See ⓦ www.ehic.org.uk for details.

OPENING HOURS

Banks ⓛ 09.00–12.30, 14.00–17.00 Mon–Fri, larger branches also 09.00–12.00 Sat

Shops ⓛ 09.30 or 10.00–12.30, 14.00–19.00 Mon–Sat

Pharmacies ⓛ 08.30 or 09.00–12.00, 14.00–19.00 Mon–Sat, larger branches also 09.00–12.30 Sun

Restaurants ⓛ 12.00–14.00, 19.00–22.30 although some are closed Mondays

Many museums are closed on Mondays; many vineyards close on Sundays (and some also on Saturdays, so call ahead).

TOILETS

There are public toilets at several places in the city centre, including along the quays, at place Paul Doumer in Chartrons and at place Stalingrad in La Bastide. There are occasionally separate ones for men and women, and most will have an entrance fee. The airport and the train station both have good public toilets, and most museums are also a good bet for clean, attractive facilities.

There are very few old-style 'hole in the ground' French toilets left in the city, and almost all are now modern European style.

CHILDREN

Bordeaux, despite its reputation for being reserved, is very child-friendly, and small children will be welcomed in almost all hotels, cafés and restaurants. Many of them provide not only high chairs but also colouring pencils and paper to keep little ones entertained. Pharmacies will sell nappies, baby food, suntan lotion and everything you might need.

On top of all that, the city has a number of fabulous attractions. For example, at Cap Sciences (see page 79), on Wednesdays, Saturdays and Sundays between June and January, there are short 'Petit Explorateur' ('Little Explorer') sessions for three- to six-year-olds, and separate ones for the five to eleven age group. The Miroir d'Eau (see page 61) is a haven for young children, especially in hot weather, where they can be kept amused for hours running in and out of the jets of water, or paddling when

⬤ The surprising Miroir d'Eau keeps everyone amused

it turns into a still, reflective (and very shallow) lake. If your little ones need to expend some energy, Ludothèque, a large play area located by the Jardin Botanique on the Right Bank is ideal, with its massive indoor and outdoor amusements. There are good playgrounds all over the city, and two are in the Jardin Public (see page 77). Older teenagers will love the Skate Park on quai des Chartrons, while kids of all ages will enjoy the **Ludothèque** (ⓐ 37 allée Jean Giono ☏ (05) 56 67 94 25 ⓦ www.ludotheque-interlude.fr ⏰ 16.00–18.00 Tues, Fri, 14.00–18.00 Wed, 14.00–17.15 Sat), a children-oriented cultural centre with a library, play area, computers, and space simply to lounge about.

COMMUNICATIONS
Internet
Bordeaux is an extensively wired (or, rather, wireless) city. Many of the bars and cafés around place des Chartrons are all Wi-Fi'd up, and there are several internet cafés on rue Notre-Dame, and lots more off place Gambetta on rue du Palais Gallien.

Phone
Card-operated public phone boxes are available across Bordeaux, and international calls can be made from them. You have to buy a *télécarte* (phonecard) at a *tabac* (newsagent's/cigarette shop). **Directory Enquires** ☏ 118712 from any phone

Post
Postal services are very reliable across France. Post offices sell telephone cards, and usually have photocopiers or a fax machine available for public use. Most have coin operated machines for

TELEPHONING BORDEAUX

The area code for southwest France is 05, followed by a number which is always eight digits in length. When dialling from anywhere in France, use all eight digits, including the 05.

To call Bordeaux numbers from outside of France, dial your own international prefix (oo in most countries) then 33 for France, then drop the initial o of the 05.

TELEPHONING ABROAD

To call abroad from France, dial oo for an international connection, then your own country code (44 for the UK, 353 Republic of Ireland, 1 USA or Canada, 61 Australia, 64 New Zealand, 27 South Africa), then the area code leaving out the intial o.

buying stamps and weighing packages if you don't want to wait in line (many French people do their banking through the post office, so queues can be long).

Post boxes are yellow and easy to spot. Stamps can be bought either from the post office or from a *tabac* (newsagent's/cigarette shop).

The two main post offices in Bordeaux are:

La Poste Bordeaux Saintonge ⓐ 2 rue Saintonge ⓣ (05) 56 99 30 80 ⓛ 08.30–18.00 Mon–Fri, 08.30–12.00 Sat

La Poste Bordeaux Tourny ⓐ 29 allées de Tourny ⓣ (05) 56 00 88 70 ⓛ 09.00–18.00 Mon–Thur, 09.00–12.00 Fri, 09.00–12.00, 14.00–18.00 Sat

ELECTRICITY

France runs on 220 volts with two-pin plugs. British appliances will need an adaptor, easily obtained at any electrical or hardware store, or at the airport. US and other equipment designed for 110 volts will need a transformer (*transformateur*).

TRAVELLERS WITH DISABILITIES

Bordeaux airport and train stations have good access points for travellers who need extra assistance, and there are lifts in most of the larger hotels. The trams have good access for people with disabilities. However, buses tend to be ill-equipped, and there are many hotels which do not have bathrooms and bedrooms that are easily adapted to wheelchairs. Useful organisations for information and advice include:

RADAR The principal UK forum and pressure group for people with disabilities. ⓐ 12 City Forum, 250 City Road, London EC1V 8AF ⓣ (020) 7250 3222 ⓦ www.radar.org.uk

SATH (Society for Accessible Travel & Hospitality) Advises US-based travellers with disabilities. ⓐ 347 Fifth Ave, Suite 610, New York NY 10016 ⓣ 212 447 7284 ⓦ www.sath.org

Association des Paralyses en France ⓐ Délégation Départementale des Alpes Maritimes, 3 avenue Antoine Véran, Nice ⓣ (04) 92 07 98 00 ⓦ www.apf.asso.fr

TOURIST INFORMATION

While in France you can reach any tourist board in the country simply by dialling 3264 from a landline and clearly stating the name of the town or city you are interested in. You will be put through automatically to the correct tourist office. Calls cost

34 cents per minute.

Maison de La France (French Tourist Board) The UK branch
can offer plenty of info before you leave. ⓐ 178 Piccadilly,
London W1J 9AL ⓣ 09068 244 123 (calls cost 60p per min)
ⓦ www.franceguide.com

Bordeaux Tourist Office ⓐ 12 cours du 30 juillet, Bordeaux
ⓣ (05) 56 00 66 00 ⓦ www.bordeaux-tourisme.com
ⓛ 09.00–19.30 Mon–Sat, 09.30–18.30 Sun, July & Aug;
09.00–19.00 Mon–Sat, 09.30–18.30 Sun, Sept–June

Saint Émilion Tourist Office ⓐ pl. des Créneaux, Saint Émilion
ⓣ (05) 57 55 28 28 ⓛ opening hours vary with the season
ⓦ www.saint-emilion-tourisme.com

Maison du Tourisme et du Vin de Pauillac ⓐ La Verrerie, Pauillac
ⓣ (05) 56 59 03 08 ⓦ www.pauillac-medoc.com ⓛ 09.30–12.30,
14.00–18.00 Mon–Sat, 10.30–12.00, 15.00–17.30 Sun

BACKGROUND READING

Bordeaux People, Power and Politics by Stephen Brook. A good
overview of Bordeaux's wine industry.

Noble Rot: A Bordeaux Wine Revolution by William Echikson.
Salacious and fascinating insight into the petty politics of
the wine world.

*Resistance and Betrayal: The Death and Life of Jean Moulin,
the Greatest Hero of the French Resistance* by Patrick Marnham.
A compelling study of a complex, hugely brave man, and
a history of the activities of the Resistance in general.

Emergencies

The following are emergency freephone numbers:
Ambulance ℹ 15
Fire & first aid ℹ 18
Police ℹ 17
All emergency services from a mobile phone ℹ 112

MEDICAL SERVICES
French medical facilities are excellent. Visitors from the UK
require a European Health Insurance Card (see page 130).
Travel insurance for health and possessions is advised.
All non-EU travellers should arrange adequate insurance.

Emergency doctors
SOS Médecins ℹ (05) 56 44 74 74 or (05) 56 99 77 77

Emergency dentist
Médico-Dentaire Health Centre ⓐ 45 rue Vital Charles
ℹ (05) 56 44 93 78 🕐 09.00–19.00 Mon–Fri, 09.00–12.00 Sat

Hospitals
Saint-André Hospital ⓐ 1 rue Jean Burguet ℹ (05) 56 79 56 79
Children's Hospital (Hôpital des Enfants) ⓐ Groupe Hospitalier
Pellegrin ℹ (05) 56 79 56 79

POLICE
Lost property ⓐ 99 rue Abbé de l'Épée ℹ (05) 56 44 20 18
🕐 08.30–16.30 Mon–Fri

EMERGENCY PHRASES

Help!   Au secours!   *Oh suhcoor!*

Call the police/fire service/ambulance!
Appelez la police/les pompiers/une ambulance!
Appeley lah police/leh pompee-eh/oon ambulance!

Police Office (main police headquarters) ⓐ 29 rue Castéja
ⓣ (05) 56 99 77 77

EMBASSIES & CONSULATES
British Consulate ⓐ 353 blvd de Président Wilson, Bordeaux
ⓣ (05) 57 22 21 10
Canadian Consulate ⓐ 10 rue Jules de Rességuier, Toulouse
ⓣ (05) 61 52 19 06 ⓛ 09.00–12.00 Mon–Fri
Spanish Consulate ⓐ 16 rue Sainte Anne, Toulouse
ⓣ (05) 34 31 96 60 ⓛ 09.00–14.00 Mon–Fri
US Consulate General ⓐ 10 pl. de la Bourse ⓣ (05) 56 48 63 80
ⓛ 09.00–14.00 Mon–Fri

Editorial/project management: Lisa Plumridge
Copy editor: Monica Guy
Layout/DTP: Alison Rayner

The publishers would like to thank the Bordeaux Tourist Office and following for supplying their copyright photographs for this book: Christian Baeur/SXC.hu, page 22; Douglas Barry, page 84; BigStockPhoto.com (Henri Frontier, pages 55 & 96; Rafael Laguillo, pages 38–9 & 113; Karine Rebora, pages 104–5); Château de Sanse, page 124; Comite Regional du Tourisme de Aquitaine/Jean-Jacques Brochard, pages 109, 117 & 122; Dreamstime.com (Hubert Coia, page 73; Claude Coquilleau, pages 31, 127 & 131; Henri Frontier, page 32; Duncan Gilbert, page 45); Fotolia.com (Phil B, pages 7 & 63; Jean-Luc Le Cuillier, page 13; Antoine Declerck, page 125; Marie Emeri, page 17; Gelinaud, page 95; Hubert, pages 41, 43 & 57; Jacques Palut, pages 26, 81 & 101; stockfoto, page 89); Mike Hanson, page 68; iStockphoto.com (John Cave, page 103; Mike Dabell, page 21; Bart De Meuter, page 5; Gregory Van Raalte, pages 28–9); Zachary Mastoon, page 47; Martha Richards, page 19; Katie Reeder, page 66; Sources de Caudalie, page 37; Frederico Spengler, page 9; untipografico, page 70.

Send your thoughts to
books@thomascook.com

- **Found a great bar, club, shop or must-see sight that we don't feature?**
- **Like to tip us off about any information that needs a little updating?**
- **Want to tell us what you love about this handy little guidebook and more importantly how we can make it even handier?**

Then here's your chance to tell all! Send us ideas, discoveries and recommendations today and then look out for your valuable input in the next edition of this title.

Email the above address (stating the title) or write to: pocket guides Series Editor, Thomas Cook Publishing, PO Box 227, Coningsby Road, Peterborough PE3 8SB, UK.

WHAT'S IN YOUR GUIDEBOOK?

Independent authors Impartial up-to-date information from our travel experts who meticulously source local knowledge.

Experience Thomas Cook's 165 years in the travel industry and guidebook publishing enriches every word with expertise you can trust.

Travel know-how Thomas Cook has thousands of staff working around the globe, all living and breathing travel.

Editors Travel-publishing professionals, pulling everything together to craft a perfect blend of words, pictures, maps and design.

You, the traveller We deliver a practical, no-nonsense approach to information, geared to how you really use it.

ABOUT THE AUTHOR

Jane Anson is a wine and travel writer based in Bordeaux, France, and author of Thomas Cook's pocket guides to Corsica and Toulouse. She is Bordeaux correspondent for *Decanter* magazine, contributing writer for the *Michelin Guide to the Wine Regions of France*, and writes regularly for *Food & Travel*, the *South China Morning Post*, *Gourmet Traveller* and a number of other international publications.

Useful phrases

English	French	*Approx pronunciation*
BASICS		
Yes	Oui	*Wee*
No	Non	*Nawng*
Please	S'il vous plaît	*Seel voo pleh*
Thank you	Merci	*Mehrsee*
Hello	Bonjour	*Bawngzhoor*
Goodbye	Au revoir	*Aw revwahr*
Excuse me	Excusez-moi	*Ekskewzeh-mwah*
Sorry	Désolé(e)	*Dehzoleh*
That's okay	Ça va	*Sahr vahr*
I don't speak French	Je ne parle pas français	*Zher ner pahrl pah frahngsay*
Do you speak English?	Parlez-vous anglais?	*Pahrlay-voo ohnglay?*
Good morning	Bonjour	*Bawng-zhoor*
Good afternoon	Bonjour	*Bawng-zhoor*
Good evening	Bonsoir	*Bawng-swah*
Goodnight	Bonne nuit	*Bun nwee*
My name is ...	Je m'appelle ...	*Zher mahpehl ...*
NUMBERS		
One	Un/Une	*Uhn/Oon*
Two	Deux	*Dur*
Three	Trois	*Trwah*
Four	Quatre	*Kahtr*
Five	Cinq	*Sank*
Six	Six	*Seess*
Seven	Sept	*Seht*
Eight	Huit	*Weet*
Nine	Neuf	*Nurf*
Ten	Dix	*Deess*
Twenty	Vingt	*Vang*
Fifty	Cinquante	*Sangkahnt*
One hundred	Cent	*Sohn*
SIGNS & NOTICES		
Airport	Aéroport	*Ahehrohpohr*
Rail station	Gare	*Gahr*
Platform	Quai	*Kay*
Smoking/ No smoking	Permit de fumer/ Interdit de fumer	*Permee der foom-eh/ Anterdee der foom-eh*
Toilets	Toilettes	*Twahlet*
Ladies/Gentlemen	Femmes/Hommes	*Fam/Ommh*
Tram/Bus	Tramway/Bus	*Tramway/Booss*